PRAISE FOR FIRE YOURSELF FIRST

Jeff Russell tackles a topic relevant to all successful entrepreneurs: Firing Yourself First. Without the freedom of time, the freedom of money doesn't mean much. Keep reading to learn how to free yourself and create a bigger future—one that you love to live every day.

—Justin Donald
#1 *Wall Street Journal* and *USA Today* Best-Selling Author
Founder of The Lifestyle Investor, and Host of
The Lifestyle Investor Podcast

In *Fire Yourself First*, Jeff gives entrepreneurs an easy-to-follow, proven process that helps them recover their time and peace of mind. The ultimate result is simple, yet powerful. They find the freedom to follow their true calling.

—Dr. Benjamin Hardy
Organizational Psychologist and Best-Selling Author

We start companies for three reasons: to accomplish something, for the money, and to give us free time. Jeff's advice about putting a key leader in place, like a COO, will not only accelerate your business, it will unchain you from the daily grind, giving you back your freedom, and a great life.

—Cameron Herold
Founder, COO Alliance
Author, *The Second In Command*

Money without freedom is like a car without wheels. It might look nice, but you won't get anywhere. Jeff's new book reveals a proven process to obtain both and leverage them to create a life you love. It all begins with Firing Yourself First. Thank you for this incredible gift.

—Kary Oberbrunner
Wall Street Journal and *USA Today*
Best-Selling Author of 12 Books

In *Fire Yourself First*, Jeff presents a clear and effective method for entrepreneurs to reclaim their time and mental well-being. The end goal is both straightforward and impactful: empowering entrepreneurs to pursue their biggest passions. Jeff genuinely embodies the principles he writes about, because he's built a business that seamlessly aligns with his ideal lifestyle, giving him the luxury of months of time off every year. Only take advice from people who have the life you want to live. Jeff is that guy!

—Mike Koenigs
Serial Entrepreneur, 13-Time #1 Best-Selling Author, Speaker, Interactive Online Personality, and Influencer

Far too often, entrepreneurs get stuck in their businesses. With his four-step blueprint, Jeff Russell teaches us how to work on our business by Firing Ourselves First. The result? A total return to freedom! Russell's book is a must-read for any high-achieving entrepreneur.

—Amy Jamrog
Wall Street Journal and *USA Today*
Best-Selling Author of *Confetti Moments*

Infused with battle-tested strategies, *Fire Yourself First* gives you a blueprint to follow so you can create an autonomous business that runs without you.

—Chad Jenkins
CEO, Charlotte Growth Partners

For entrepreneurs seeking a fulfilling life and thriving business on their own terms, *Fire Yourself First* is a must-read book full of practical strategies and valuable insights.

—Lori Ell, CPA, CMA, ICD.D
Founder and President, Growing Ideas
Vistage/TEC Master Chair

Jeff provides clear, easy steps to rise above just running your business and leveraging your hard work to achieve freedom and happiness.

—Matt Faure
President and CEO, Trimac Transportation

Fire Yourself First is the perfect blueprint for the entrepreneur or business owner who wants to realize the benefits of all the hard work invested and sacrificed over the years to create a special organization and the opportunity to enjoy the freedom and a fulfilled life. Jeff talks about creating a culture of empowerment. By surrounding yourself with character individuals who are competent and caring, you create a leadership team and organization that allows you to make yourself redundant in the day-to-day operation and prioritize your role on the strategy to enhance your business and to ensure you are living your best life. Jeff teaches us that though the financial rewards and benefits that originally may have driven our passion are important, understanding the freedom of a healthy lifestyle is more so. Internal happiness can end up being the real benefit of *Fire Yourself First*. A great read for anyone who desires to have both.

—Allan J. Klassen
Chief Experience Officer, Brookfield Properties Development

FIRE YOURSELF FIRST

FIRE YOURSELF FIRST

Unchain Yourself from The Daily Grind, Create an Autonomous Business, and Do What You Love Next

Jeff Russell

ethos
collective

Published by Ethos Collective™
PO Box 43
Powell, OH 43065

Library of Congress Control Number: 2023904838

Softcover: 978-1-63680-143-8
Hardcover: 978-1-63680-144-5
E-book: 978-1-63680-145-2

Available in hardcover, softcover, audiobook and e-book.

Dedication

To the thousands of entrepreneurs I've had the opportunity to learn from throughout my life. You all contributed to this book and taught me to *live a life well lived* through your wisdom.

CONTENTS

*Creating a business that runs without you gives you
the freedom to choose a life you love.*

Part Three: Do What You Love Next

Note to the Reader

Just as everyone has different tastes in music and movies, people also have different desires when they read a book. There are some who take in every single line and who read every single page (including the dedication). Then, there are those who want to dive right into the heart of the material and just want to know precisely what they must do to Fire Themselves First.

I'll honor those of you who only want to learn the facts by giving you the option of skipping over Part 1 and heading over to Part 2, which lays out my 4-step process to Fire Yourself First. While you'll definitely save yourself some time by skipping Part 1, just know you'll also miss out on my explanation of *who* needs to Fire Themselves First and *what* it means to do so. Part 1 also includes my backstory of how I learned to Fire Myself First, and I share some valuable insights I've learned along my personal journey.

Whether you start with Part 1 or Part 2, I can't wait for you to begin the journey of *firing yourself first*, gaining the tools needed to unchain yourself from your business to have the kind of life you've always dreamed of living.

Jeff Russell

PART ONE

Unchain Yourself from Your Business

Why We Need to Fire Ourselves First

S arah never showed up to the event. She had planned to be there, paid money for her ticket, and yet her seat remained empty. Her lonely chair was an ominous, silent warning, and it left me wondering what had happened. Perhaps there had been a family emergency? Perhaps she'd gotten tied up at work? What had caused this woman, a hardworking physician who had made her way through medical school and put in long hours, to fail to show? Later I discovered the cause of her absence—suicide. Sadly, Sarah had killed herself just days before the event. But what drove this woman, someone who was known for helping to save lives, to take her own?

While Sarah's case is an extraordinary one, unfortunately, there are many people out there just like her—ambitious, entrepreneurial, and hardworking—yet something is drastically wrong. Like Sarah, many people find themselves unhappy or even miserable because they are overworked and stretched too thin. Whether their worlds disintegrate into divorce, another kind of loss, or in Sarah's case—suicide—many find themselves working too much, stressing too much, and losing too much in the process. I've noticed this pattern over the years while putting on my live events where I teach doctors how to increase revenues at their practices. Along the way, I've discovered that my events sell out precisely because many of these frontline healthcare workers are fed up with being worked too hard without receiving any recognition. The result is they desire to escape their current workplace pain by leaving traditional medicine. They hope to enter the field of private, cash-pay medicine because, for them, that's where they might find some workplace happiness.

Have you noticed the common thread between Sarah's story and these frontline doctors? These are all individuals who find themselves chained to their work, wanting their time back, wanting their lives back, but they aren't sure how to do so. Unfortunately, they are not alone. Multiple studies on stress have shown that the workplace, without a doubt, is one of the largest sources of stress. In fact, 7 out of 10 adults reported that workplace stress affected their personal relationships, and the amount of work on one's plate was the most commonly reported cause of workplace stress.[1] One study even noted that 70% of all doctor's visits are linked to workplace stress. No matter how you slice it, people are stressed, and they are stressed about work.

While you're not alone in feeling overwhelmed by work, you're also not on your own when it comes to a solution. In *Fire Yourself First*, I'm here to show you how to unchain yourself from your work and create an autonomous business that runs without you in order to free up your time so you can do what you love. While it's taken me many years to develop this system, my four-part plan enabled me to do just that—break the chains linking me to my business and get my life back. When I did so, I found that I had the freedom to think about what I truly wanted from my life while simultaneously having the time to pursue it.

In *Fire Yourself First*, I'm here to show you how to unchain yourself from your work and create an autonomous business that runs without you in order to free up your time so you can do what you love.

Who Needs to Fire Themselves First?

At first glance, the title of the book—*Fire Yourself First*—actually sounds a bit threatening and possibly even menacing. For those of you who already own or operate a company, you might wonder why on earth you would want to fire yourself?

What would you do?

What would your company do without you?

How would your family react?

What would your friends and colleagues say?

Well, if you did it right, then they should congratulate you!

In essence, *Fire Yourself First* is a business owner's guide that provides entrepreneurs with an operating system that will allow your business to grow, while simultaneously reducing the amount of time you spend working on it. It's a system for those looking to eventually sell their businesses for the highest price, and it's also for those seeking peace of mind—who want to take a step back from the rat race—and desire to spend only several hours a month running the business. It's also a system for business owners endeavoring to set up their company to run without them, so they can do what fulfills them. If any of those descriptions sound like you, then you need to fire yourself first.

When considering your business, if you can't leave it for a day, then my Fire Yourself First Process™ is for you. If you need to work on your business for more than ten hours a month, it's also for you. It's important to note that *Fire Yourself First* is not meant to be a tactical strategy book on how to sell your business or about the day-to-day operations of running a business. (If your business is struggling operation-wise, you should start implementing this book's strategies because it is always better to start earlier. However, I'd recommend doing additional research and work on your operating systems. For example, one of the best business operating systems I've come across is the Entrepreneurial Operating System®, or EOS®, by Gino Wickman, and he also has a great book, *Traction: Get a Grip on Your Business*.) The concepts found within the pages of this book are designed for the business owner who already has a successful business, with the processes and systems already in place. What's missing, however, are the processes and systems that enable you to have a business run *without* you.

This book, then, will help owner entrepreneurs set up my four-part system so the business can actually run without them, freeing them up for the other things that life has to offer. Ultimately, my purpose is to free up your time, which will help you rethink your life and your purpose, and then help you create the concrete steps leading you to the life you've always wanted to live. It's what I call "How to Live a Life Well Lived."

Maybe you remain skeptical because you haven't yet reached that point in your business. For the time being, you're enjoying the grind, and these words about workplace stress, lack of purpose, and wanting to sell the business all seem an unnecessary warning.

I get it.

There is a time when business owners and entrepreneurs love working in their business and being an integral part of its operations. In fact, this is what gets them out of bed in the morning and keeps them excited throughout the day.

However, even if you're not there yet, even if you haven't felt like you're starting to lose your life, lose your family, or just plain lose it, one day, you might understand what I'm talking about. There may come a time when the business no longer excites you. You may start thinking of selling or scaling back your involvement. Possibly you've reached that point where you find yourself running on a hamster wheel, going around and around, yet not moving forward. To make matters worse, you don't know how to get off of the wheel even though you are desperate to do so. The demands of the business may be causing you to miss commitments to family or friends and you find your personal life suffering along with your mental state. Whether you're there now or wind up at this point in your business later, you don't have to stay there. Fortunately, this book will show you another way.

A Better Way

In the beautiful, desert town of Sedona, Arizona there are a plethora of hiking paths that enable one to take in the gorgeous red rock scenery, arches, and hidden caves. As I've hiked Sedona's terrain, I've noticed how many paths I can choose from. Sometimes the hiking trail is clearly marked, other times it's not. In those moments, it might be tricky deciding which path to take because no one wants to end up lost or, even worse, in danger. In a similar way, maybe you have been going down the wrong business path over and over again, a path that has left you wondering what your purpose is and what you should be doing with your life. In those moments, what you truly need is a guide. In hiking, the value of any good guide is that he or she can get you to where you want to be quicker and safer. That's what I offer to you: the opportunity to get where you'd like to be using my expertise of having already done so myself. This is a trail I've already blazed, and I'm here to serve as your guide, taking you onto a different, better path—a path that you never knew existed.

Many entrepreneurs haven't yet discovered another way. They haven't realized that we don't have to be stuck in the daily grind, chained to our businesses, stressed out of our minds, wondering when this nightmare will finally be over, and working ourselves to death. Many entrepreneurs feel shackled by the same business that was supposed to give them freedom. The good news is they aren't stuck in their current situation. Other, and better, ways available. It doesn't matter whether you're a school-aged kid, a college student, an executive, or even a CEO or founder of a company— there is another way to live. I'm here to show you what's possible.

As a business owner, I know that every entrepreneur dreams of having both financial freedom and a lifestyle of freedom. In other words, we desire a life that gives us freedom *from* something and gives us freedom *for* something else. So, how do we gain that freedom we crave? How do we stop being overworked and overstressed? Put simply, by creating an autonomous or self-running company that we can scale to whatever level we dream of. Once this autonomous business is in place, it will run on its own, generating income while simultaneously giving you the free time to imagine, create, and focus on your own personal evolution. In short, you gain freedom from work and freedom to dream.

Think about autonomous vehicles. Today, several companies, including Tesla™, offer the public a chance to buy self-driving (or semi-autonomous) cars.

> Once this autonomous business is in place, it will run on its own, generating income while simultaneously giving you the free time to imagine, create, and focus on your own personal evolution.

These vehicles are capable of sensing the environment and operating without much human involvement. They rely on sensors, actuators, complex algorithms, machine learning systems, and powerful processors to execute software.[2] In other words, when you own a self-driving car, the car can drive itself in most or all situations, even though a human passenger must be ready to take control if need be. Similarly, it's possible for you to set up your business in the same way, where it runs on its own without much involvement from you, the owner.

What Does it Mean to Fire Yourself First?

To achieve this freedom and walk this new, better path, we have to do something we have possibly never thought of—we need to fire *ourselves* first. We need to realize maybe what's wrong with our business is our own role in it. We are what is wrong. Perhaps we are doing too much, not hiring the right people, or lacking the right systems in place. As such, we need to fire ourselves first, which is simply putting into place the systems that will allow us to take a step or two away from the business. In doing so, we still maintain the ability to run our business but without its current demands on our time. In the end, we take ourselves out of the equation, while maintaining a functioning, profitable business and lessening its demands on our lives.

There's a common expression that resonates with me:

Give a man a fish, and you feed him for a day. Teach a man to fish, and you feed him for a lifetime.

This popular adage, in a sense, sums up the purpose of my book. I'm trying to teach you *how* to fish—*how* to create an autonomous business that runs on its own to free you up for what you really would like to do in life. I don't just want to give you a proverbial fish that leads to a life of you working yourself to death. No, I desire to teach you *how* to fish—how to set up your business in a way that lends itself to producing more and more income for you while providing you the opportunity to pursue something else with your life.

This is the path I'm offering you. It's the other way and the better way—where you can work less and make the same (or potentially even more) money. It's the path that unchains you from your business. It's the path that offers you freedom.

For example, did you know it was possible to only work ten days a month or a few days a week, freeing you up to spend your time (and your life) on what you *truly* want? That is the current situation I'm in, which should show you that it's possible. It's possible to be free from the long hours and the grind. It's possible to get off of the hamster wheel. In fact, my story could one day be your story. I'm not special or different. I simply implemented the process.

Begin at the End: Six Feet Under, the ATM, or the Sale

Back in 1989, Stephen R. Covey wrote the famous self-help book *The Seven Habits of Highly Effective People*. The first habit was "be proactive," which obviously you are, or you wouldn't be in the position you are today. However, we often forget about the second habit: "begin with the end in mind."[3] For instance, did you wake up this morning thinking about the end of the day, your business, or even your life? While many are not going to like the reality of that statement, the truth is, everyone is going to exit his or her business at some point in time. In fact, we are all going to end up six feet under. That is the end game we are all playing. So, if we think about that eventuality, that inevitability, how would you critique the life you are living today? Are you truly doing what is most important? Are you the person you want to be to your team members, colleagues, friends, and family? When it comes to your business, can you walk away from it and still maintain the quality of life you have now? If the answer to that question is no, then now is the time to make it right because if you can't leave your business, then how are you going to live the life you have always imagined?

Most people go through various phases of their business, and they become stuck in one. For instance, when you start a business, whether you are the CEO or founder, you go through the start-up phase. Eventually, you move into a scaling or growth phase. Then possibly you add a new product or service to the business, which takes you back to the start-up phase again for a bit. At some point, you might head into a systems or processes phase, where you document what is working and fix what isn't. With those systems in place, you could then find yourself moving back into the scaling phase. And so, the business cycles on and on. It seems that just when you've started to sleep well, there's always something else that you need to be planning for or keeps you worried. You may find yourself worried about a recession or whether a new product or service will create a liability issue. What about a pandemic? What about an economic collapse? What if the world's geo-politics undergo a massive change?

This is why it's important to begin with the end in mind. We must remember that, at some point, we will all exit our businesses. We might exit because we are six feet under, we might exit because we've reduced our time and have enabled the business to operate without us, or we might exit because we have sold the company. In fact, all three of these should happen, but hopefully not in that order.

When we begin with the end in mind, we realize the order those steps *should* occur. The first step is to create your business in a way that it will run without you. In other words, you have created an autonomous business. When you do so, you give yourself the choice of how much time you want to spend working on the business each month. I like to think of this as the ATM stage. Just like an ATM that we pull up to, insert our bank card, and receive our cash, in this step, your business is working hard on your behalf with you having to work too much, and it continues to generate cash for you, day after day, year after year. In essence, your business is your own private ATM—you receive cash without much effort. While perhaps the ATM is a bit of a crude metaphor, it helps us understand what we are trying to do with our businesses. We're trying to create a business so that, like an ATM running by itself with little outside maintenance, we can step away from it knowing that the business will continue to operate and give us the freedom to pursue what we truly care about.

Once the business operates on its own, we move to the next possible stage: the sale. For many entrepreneurs, selling is their goal. They want a big check and use that money to live the life they've always wanted. If you decide to sell your business, you will benefit greatly from having already reached the ATM stage. This is because what gives you the ability to sell your business at the highest valuation is that your business does not depend on you to run it. Buyers aren't interested in a business that requires the presence of its former owner. Thus, in some strange way, a business you dreamt up and created will be worth more once you're out of the picture. When we understand that our businesses will sell better at the ATM stage, we realize the importance of beginning with the end in mind when creating an autonomous business.

When it comes to selling, of all the businesses, only 10% successfully sell, which is an abysmal fact.[4] If your business relies on you, that is, you are critical to its success, then your business is unsellable. In other words, you are trapped. This is the reason to fire yourself first. Here's a quick question to check if your business is sellable: can it run without you? If it can't, then now is the time to begin the process of firing yourself first. Remember, if your business can't run

> **Remember, if your business can't run without you, if you can't step away from it for a few weeks and have it operate without you, then you don't have a business—you have a job.**

without you, if you can't step away from it for a few weeks and have it operate without you, then you don't have a business—you have a job. If you want to have a true business, it needs to run with or without you.

There are both pros and cons to creating the ATM and selling the business. For those who create the ATM, you still have the opportunity to keep your mind active and solve problems. This option is for those excited about creating long-term business strategies and maintaining a great culture. These are the individuals who want to stay involved but limit their day-to-day involvement. However, if you're in the ATM stage, then remember, you still have to deal with the problems that come along with the business. On the other hand, if you find yourself lacking peace and failing to enjoy life, then selling may be the best option for you. The good news is regardless of which path you choose, the process remains the same. Even if you want to sell, you will receive a greater valuation on your business if your involvement is not integral to the operation of the company. The more essential your role in the business, the less valuable you are to a prospective buyer. Either way—whether you create the ATM or you create the ATM and then sell—you need to recognize for entrepreneurs, owning a business is much more than just a career. You're also on a deeper journey here. It's not like working for a big company where you are a cog in a big machine. What you do with your businesses is personal, and you must remember the key for every successful business exit is to fire yourself first!

This takes us to the third stage: six feet under. By achieving the ability to sell your business at the highest possible valuation, you and your family will be taken care of when it's your time to leave this world. Although death might not be the happiest of thoughts, you need to always begin with the end in mind. This helps you take steps in the right order when it comes to setting up yourself and your loved ones for success.

In the end, I want you to think about the big picture.

- What do you really want?
- Where do you want to be in fifteen years?
- What do you want to be doing?
- What do you want the exit of your business life to look like?
- Do you want to keep your business and simply have it run without you?
- Are you more interested in getting your business to the ATM stage so that you will improve the company's valuation and be prepared to sell sooner rather than later?
- What kind of life do you want to live?
- More importantly, how do you live a life well lived?

Ultimately, *Fire Yourself First* will help you to focus on your owner's mindset.

Signs of Struggle

For those entrepreneurs still wondering whether or not they should fire themselves first and unchain themselves from their businesses, a good way to start is to ask yourself a few questions:

- Are you frustrated with your business and lack a sense of purpose?
- Do you feel overwhelmed and overworked?
- Do you lack a clear exit strategy?
- Do you find yourself wondering what's next?
- Are you looking for a higher purpose in life and wanting to walk the path of self-discovery?

Here's an analogy that drives the point home and it has to do with food. I love to barbeque, but there is a point in the cooking process when your pork butt or brisket "stalls." Up until the point of stalling, things are going well, and then BAM: three or four hours in, the internal temperature of the meat hits about 145 degrees Fahrenheit and won't budge. It has, in fact, stalled. It's a disheartening moment, especially since this stall can last anywhere from two to three hours. However, at some point, the meat breaks through the stall and away it goes! The temperature works its way up to 205 degrees Fahrenheit, and you're ready to enjoy dinner.

Similarly, there are many entrepreneurs experiencing their first "stall" in their business or in life. Things may have been going well for a while, but suddenly, they feel that something is missing. They have realized that what they are doing isn't working and, despite their best efforts, they feel a need to change. They need help, and they've accepted they need help–they are genuinely ready to listen. These individuals want more for themselves, their families, and the other important people in their lives. They have, in effect, "stalled" and they are looking for a way to reach the end. It's time to break through that workplace stall and how to see what you don't see.

Over the years, I've observed many entrepreneurs crushed by the demands of their companies. Sadly, they believe the only way to get out from underneath the weight of their business is to sell. In their minds, selling is the only escape plan. The truth is there's another way. You can create a self-running business (your ATM) that enables you to remain a part of the business while you are apart from the business. Then, when the day finally comes to sell, you can sell because you *want* to, and on your terms, not because you think it's the only option.

A Call to Freedom

In your journey, I'd be honored to be your guide, someone who can show you the path to the freedom that's out there. I want you to live the life you've always dreamed of living, whether that's pursuing philanthropic work halfway across the globe or simply spending more time with your grand-children in your backyard. This reality is attainable because, for the first time, the demands of work have lessened and you have time, free time, on your hands. Imagine a world where you are happy with the effortlessness of your profes-sional and personal life.

In Part Two of the book, we will explore a simple, four-step system that will enable you to create an auton-omous business setting yourself up to sell your business at its highest valuation. Finally, in Part Three, we will discuss what's next—what do we do once we've unchained ourselves.

If you've ever found yourself wondering, "What's next for me?" but feel unable to leave the business, *Fire Yourself First* will teach you how to get your time back. Even more, it will teach you how to get your life back.

Learning the Hard Way

How did I find a way to work only ten days a month and unshackle myself from my companies? Well, at my core, I am a problem solver. Once, another executive told me that if she were alone on a desert island and only had one person to call, she would call me. Why? She felt I would be able to come up with a solution to any problem she encountered. To find my own free time, I put my problem-solving skills to use and discovered how to unchain myself from my own business. Somewhere along my entrepreneurial path, I learned that making money for money's sake didn't excite me. It just didn't float my boat, so to speak. So, what excites me? Giving someone else his or her "aha moment." I find fulfillment helping others, and thankfully, because I am unchained from my businesses, I now have the time to help others and lead them to their own eye-opening moments. In fact, that's my vision for my current work life: I work a total of ten days a month and spend the other days doing whatever it is that I want, which includes reading and helping others. Even though this process of learning how to fire myself first didn't happen overnight, I was eventually able to do so and I know you can too.

My Path to Freedom

I began my life as an entrepreneur when I created my own business, Oakridge Financial Group, from my basement, and I ended up turning it into a multimillion-dollar business. I fully ran it until I began to slowly hire others. For a while, the business was not running without me, and scale was certainly an issue because it was limited to how many calls I could make, how many deals I could transact, and so on. However, this is where I first entered the business waters, and I still had much to learn.

My second business derived from the first, as I started training physicians how to start a private medical practice and incorporate aesthetic medical procedures. It was during this second business that I brought in medical experts, as the company provided cosmetic medical procedure training and. Because I was not a physician, I needed to hire doctors who could train others in those areas while I trained them in the area of my expertise—running their businesses. Despite having hired various people, I had still made myself indispensable to this second business for the first ten years. But my status as a critical cog in the business machine was about to change.

So, how did I discover the Fire Yourself First Process? To be honest, it was quite by accident. The process all began when I started my third business in 2010, a medical clinic that performed cosmetic and medical weight loss procedures. It was upon starting this business I purposely used everything I had previously learned and made it a lifestyle business. For me, the term "lifestyle business" simply means a business I enjoy because I don't work on it for more than one or two hours a month. This was an entirely new way of doing business, and it changed everything for me.

When my partner and I opened the medical clinic, we both had full-time jobs and weren't looking for another full-time gig. So, we set up the clinic with the understanding that we would each need to work only a few hours a month. In order to do this, I created a training manual on business operations I could give to someone in the clinic. At the time, I was inspired by the franchise system, where you are given an enormous binder that shows you how to operate a business. Accordingly, I documented every process in our clinic business, including phone scripts, opening procedures, and everything else that happened during the day's operations. Once we had documented the operations, we needed to hire people to execute our clinic's operations. However, simply hiring the right people wasn't enough.

I quickly discovered when you're not in the business day-to-day, as the owner, you still need to know what is going on. That's when I developed my key metrics concerning business operations. By quickly reviewing these numbers, I could gauge the health of the clinic even if I wasn't there every day. I also knew if my business partner and I ever wanted to sell the business, the clinic's value would be higher if it did not require either of us to run it. So, as a bonus, not only did we connect the key metrics to our business strategy, but we also improved our business's valuation exponentially by having a system of processes, our key metrics, and a team in place that could run the business without us.

In the end, when I contemplated those key processes that allowed me to step away from the business, I realized it came down to having a team in place to execute clearly documented systems and processes. As a result, the clinic employees knew what winning looks like, as did the team we'd put together to run it, and my partner and I were able to track our winning by using the key numbers that showed whether we were growing and continuing to grow. Getting everyone on board is critical to a company's success, but unfortunately, according to a study published in the *Harvard Business Review*, only 5% of employees understand their company's strategy.[5] The fact is most employees don't know what winning looks like, and remember, without a team in place to execute the daily operations, you'll never be able to unshackle yourself from your business.

The Evolution of My Business Systems

Although I had success in my third business and had learned how to free myself from the day-to-day operations of the company, I didn't stop there. I took these same processes I learned—the operating procedures, the team, and the key numbers—and I put them to work in another company I owned. In doing so, I learned that these processes worked quite well there also. However, I didn't achieve overnight success. It took ten years.

As I worked to apply these systems to one of my other businesses, I went through many years of experimenting, clarifying, and creating new numbers to ensure that the key metrics were accurate (not to mention hiring and rehiring to find the right team members). It truly was a marathon and not a sprint. Still, what I learned is these same concepts, the initial concepts I discovered through my clinic business, were applicable to different businesses and industries, and that was powerful information. Knowing this information led me on yet another path in my business life—now I could help others in their own businesses. Now I could share advice, strategies, procedures, and best practices with others.

That's one of the beauties of this system—you can apply it to other fields. For example, over the last sixteen years, I've helped over ten thousand physicians open up private medical practices by giving them the tools they need to operate their clinics without being present in the day-to-day. In addition, the concepts in Part Two of *Fire Yourself First* have already been taught to over three thousand business owners.

Repurpose Your Past Experience

Because I came from corporate America, I already knew many of the best practices for running a larger business, but when I began my life as an entrepreneur, what I didn't know were the intricacies of starting a small business. I knew the startup business failure rate and was determined I would not be in that statistic. So, how did I ensure I wasn't one of those startup failures?

Thankfully, throughout my life, I've always read a lot of books, and I've also loved going to the library. When I was a young child, my set of encyclopedias fascinated me. I wanted to read them again and again. In essence, I've always loved to learn. It's no surprise that I read many business books along my entrepreneurial journey.

As I read, what I was really learning, unbeknownst to me, was how to run and sustain the most efficient business. For instance, I learned if you wanted to scale your company, you needed to have systems in place. Naturally, I focused on reading books on systemization so I could learn to do it myself. In addition to scaling the business, I also discovered, after the systems were in place, I was actually building a business that would run by itself. This was ultimately what I had always wanted because if my businesses couldn't run without me, then I simply had a job, even if my title was founder, CEO, and president. However, if I could implement various systems to make my company run without me, then I would have the freedom to make as much money as possible without having any living limitations or ceilings. It was a dream come true.

In addition to reading business book after business book, I joined business groups, such as Vistage, Strategic Coach®, Genius Network®, and the Chamber of Commerce, to connect with and learn from other business owners. I also contemplated what I had learned from prior job experiences. For example, one of my previous roles was with Fairmont Hotels, and one of our key metrics was to have a 50 percent profit margin. In my role there, I saw the comfort and growth that profit margin allowed us, so a 50 percent profit margin became a key metric in my own businesses. (We will cover these key numbers more in Part Two of the book).

The point is that I was taking everything I had learned—from previous jobs, reading over one thousand business books, doing business coaching, and becoming a member of high-level networking groups—to create systems that would help me run my own businesses. I immersed myself in the deep waters, studying the best practices for starting and running my own business, and all this work gave me the tools to fire myself first.

Along the way, I also discovered something about myself. I am someone who needs to "do" in order to learn, so I was very much deep in the weeds as I created, tested, and executed the business systems and processes I'd discovered. As the years progressed, I used these systems to enable me to work less while simultaneously making more money. It was at that point that I started teaching my systems and pro-cesses to other startup businesses. My goal was to create a life where I had the freedom of both time and money to do what I wanted. Thus, my stubbornness about having the life I wanted was the catalyst that propelled me towards culti-vating the lifestyle I wanted. As a side benefit, I managed to create a simple set of processes that other entrepreneurs could implement so they could also live the lifestyle they've always wanted.

Another Thing I've Learned: Our Experience Matters

Have you ever left a restaurant or a theater and felt exhil-arated? Whether the waiter was excellent, the food was delicious, or perhaps the décor was stunning, you had a wonderful experience, and it made you want to return again and again. Why? Because *how* we experience something matters. Personally, I like going to restaurants with bars and enjoy meeting the bartenders and other patrons. In fact, I generally prefer to sit at the kitchen bar, so I can see what's going on and interact with both the staff and fellow patrons alike. It gives me a chance to ask them questions and learn about them.

I remember all of their names (okay, so I use my Notes app to keep track of them all), but I love it when I enter a place and I know them, and they know me. It's my modern-day *Cheers* moment. While not all bars are like this, it's these kinds of places that matter to me. These are the ones I return to again and again because I am fascinated by the experience they create, an experience that I enjoy and that makes me feel special. Why? Because our experience matters. It matters at a restaurant, it matters in the work-place, and it matters in life. As humans, we value experience, and when it comes to our workplace, we're not going to be satisfied with our businesses if we are not enjoying our lives because how we *experience* life, what we do day in and day out, matters.

When I worked as a dj for Club Med in the Bahamas, part of my job was to create an experience for our guests. Later, when I worked for Fairmont Hotels, we emphasized creating experiences for our guests, and we excelled at doing so. Because we understood that how people experience something matters. Even today, when it comes to my own work environment, I desire an atmosphere that is calm yet simultaneously exciting and beautiful. In fact, all my current live events take place at a resort in Scottsdale, Arizona, because people seem to learn better when they are out of their usual environment.

We need to apply this same concept to how we run and craft our businesses. Are you creating a world where you're a hamster running on a wheel or are you doing something different, something that creates a life you've always dreamed of living? Ask yourself what kind of experience your business is creating for your life. Does something need to change? If so, that's what Part Two is all about teaching you the systems that will enable you to unshackle yourself from your business because how we work and how we experience life matter.

> **Are you creating a world where you're a hamster running on a wheel or are you doing something different, something that creates a life you've always dreamed of living?**

Fire Yourself First 4-Step Process™

As mentioned, in Part Two we'll unpack the four steps that will enable you to fire yourself first, but before we begin, here is a quick summary of the steps.

Step 1: Unearthing Your Personal Why: *To find your way, you must first find your why.*

Step 2: Hiring Your Autonomous Team (The 11-step Hiring Process): *To experience true independence, your team must work independently of you.*

Step 3: Dashboards & Scorecards: *You'll never know if you're winning if you never keep score.*

Step 4: Your Autonomous Exit: *Creating a business that runs without you gives you the freedom to choose a life you love.*

PART TWO

Create Your Self-Running Systems

STEP 1

Unearthing Your Personal Why

To find your way, you must first find your why.

H ave you ever put something together, such as a child's dollhouse, and the building process drove you nuts? There were so many pieces and such detailed instructions that you found yourself wondering who designed this wicked contraption? Have you ever called in to speak with a customer service representative only to be met by an automated response that told you to press three for this option, which led you to another menu, and so on? Maybe you were so annoyed that you hung up the phone.

Why are these situations so universally frustrating? It's because we all want to get to the point. We desire a straight path, and we don't want complicated systems in our life. I am no exception to this principle, consequently, when I designed the Fire Yourself First Process, my goal was to create a simple, four-part system to guide you down the path of firing yourself first. It's not complicated or tricky, but it is meant to be life-giving.

By following the Fire Yourself First Process, you're putting systems into place that will enable your business to run without you. So, whether you desire to exit your business or run it as an ATM, your company will have all of the tools it needs to continue to run efficiently after you've gone.

It's important to note before you can even begin the journey of firing yourself first, your business must already be running well. In other words, your company needs to be consistently executing its deliverables to customers. In addition, your company should be operating at the highest efficiencies, earning you the highest profit with the lowest expenses paid.

On the flip side, your company is not ready if you struggle with any of these red flags:

1. If you're having trouble making payroll.
2. If your business operating expenses are too high.
3. If you have inconsistent revenue or customers who don't pay at all.
4. If your business is keeping you up at night with worry.

The common thread among these businesses that aren't quite ready is that the company's operating systems aren't working properly. To fire yourself first, your company's operating processes must be in place, otherwise you haven't earned the freedom to not be around. However, if your business has reached operational excellence, then congratulations! Your company is ready and able for you to begin the journey of firing yourself first.

In the words of bestselling author Simon Sinek, "It starts with why."

Step 1: Unearthing Your Personal Why

Whenever we use any kind of app to help us with directions, we tend to focus on our desired destination. However, equally important as that final destination is taking into consideration our current location or where we're starting from. We need to apply that same concept when it comes to firing ourselves first. Thus, the first step in the Fire Yourself First Process is to start with where you are right now, and ask yourself, "Am I ready?"

For many people, this first step is the most challenging one of the entire process because they've never taken the time to stop and ponder their lives. The truth is, when you're asking yourself whether you're ready, what you're *really* asking yourself is *why* you're doing this.

- Are you delving into the Fire Yourself First Process so you can exit your business?
- Is your aim to scale yourself out of the business?
- Where do you hope to end up after implementing the program?

In short, before you can decide which direction to take, it's imperative to know your why. Ask, "Why am I doing what I am doing?" Once you understand your why you'll discover the purpose behind what you're doing, and that purpose is going to help guide you throughout the remainder of the process.

It's interesting to note that knowing your personal why is a critical part of a successful business exit because the last thing you want to do is scale down the time that you spend on your business or even sell it, only to be unhappy afterward.

Over the years, one of the things I've heard from people who have exited their businesses is that they now feel lost or aren't sure what to do next. These individuals were caught up in the euphoria of having their financial goals met, but unfortunately, they forgot to contemplate what they were going to do with their newfound freedom and time. Unfortunately, what was supposed to be a blessing turned into a problem of not knowing what to do with all of the extra time and all of the extra money. Simply put, they hadn't taken the time to contemplate what would come next for them, and that missed step created a bit of chaos once they exited their businesses.

Bo Burlingham recognizes the great sense of loss that business owners can undergo when they leave their companies. In his book, *Finish Big: How Great Entrepreneurs Exit Their Companies on Top*, Burlingham writes:

> When you sell a company people lose four things: their identity, their purpose, their sense of achievement, and their network of personal connection from the people in their company both individually and collectively.[6]

What Burlingham is simply saying is that these people are lost in their new lives apart from their companies, and I don't want that to be you. The fact is, it would be rather easy to skip ahead in this process and begin at step 2 of the Fire Yourself First Process and then move on to steps 3 and 4. While skipping ahead and implementing the other tools would certainly make your company run more smoothly and efficiently, it wouldn't be wise. It is so important to slow down and start at the very beginning with step 1. You must take the time to understand why you are doing this. For me, I was determined to understand my personal why, so I read

Sinek's book and even completed his workbook. From there, it took me about two to three months to completely figure out my personal why. But then it happened—I discovered that my personal why is focusing on others.

> How can I contribute to others?
> How can I give back?
> How do I implement my personal why—my desire to help others—into my life?

Understanding my personal why brought much clarity to my life and enabled me to see the kinds of things I should be engaging in with my free time. For example, one way of giving back is through teaching others how to fire themselves first, so they, too, can gain freedom and live a life well lived. Along the way, I've also been able to contribute to others by helping high school business students and serving at a homeless food kitchen. All those actions are a product of my personal why. To this day, I contribute wherever I can because I know, without a doubt, what is important to me. Once you discover your own why, you'll be able to create future goals that you look forward to accomplishing. It's invigorating to discover your life after your business. It's like getting a second wind in life.

The Journey of Finding My Purpose

We've all heard the phrase, "Be careful what you wish for." This admonition serves as a reminder that often what we dream about having can potentially hurt us in the end. It's the same with exiting our businesses—we must be careful to uncover our purpose (our personal why) so the blessings of exiting don't become sources of pain. By nature, I am a thinker, and I often find myself contemplating life and asking questions such as, "What do I want?" and "Is this all there is?" It was during those moments of reflection that I unearthed my greatest discovery—my purpose in life. It was in contemplating what life was all about that I learned so much about myself. For instance, I discovered I was the type of person who didn't want to play golf nor did I want to spend my days sunning on the beach. That didn't excite me, but neither did I want to spend my time sitting in cafes and drinking coffee day after day. I was the kind of person who wanted to keep my mind busy and I wanted to help people. I wanted to find my why and it took time, along with a meeting with Mike Koenigs, to figure that out.

When I met Mike, he helped me to think outside of the box. He asked me questions about what I can do, what I'm good at, and what's my superpower. I always knew my Unique Ability® was being able to simplify the complex and create systems and processes that run efficiently. However, *because* those things came so naturally to me, I didn't think much about them. To be honest, they didn't seem like anything special. However, when I honestly contemplated my strengths and gifts, I realized I could utilize those systems and processes I'd designed to create an autonomous business. Then, I'd be able to work only a few hours a month while still maintaining my business. That ability—to design a business in such a way that you could run it without having to work much—seemed very important because, when you think about it, how many CEOs and business founders take calls at lunchtime? How many don't take a vacation?

In the end, it was Mike who connected my past experiences, my expertise, and my passions. Through my conversations with him, I discovered running a business is my zone of expertise, as is running a business training company and running multiple businesses in different industries. However, the area I loved deeply and where I excelled was in helping others get to where I was too. It was a significant discovery to realize I could help others create autonomous businesses (or run with minimal involvement), which would free them up for whatever it is that they wanted to do next: charitable work, pursuing additional education, traveling, mentoring others, or whatever they wanted. Thus, my personal why took a while to curate and I needed some help from others, but it has been consistent for over ten years now.

In a sentence my why is: I desire to make a positive difference in people's lives by encouraging them to see beyond what they can see now by serving as their guide.

I first *found* my purpose. Then, I used my businesses to *fund* my purpose. The truth is, I found more joy in contributing to or helping someone else. Because this was my personal why, I used my businesses to cash flow the work I wanted to do for others. That's how, for example, I could use money generated from my businesses to build orphanages in India. And that's what I want for

> I first *found* my purpose. Then, I used my businesses to *fund* my purpose.

you—I want you to discover your own personal why, so you can live the life you've always dreamed of.

The End Game Clarity Map™

While taking any journey, there's nothing like a good map to guide us and help us anticipate the twists and turns along the way. When it comes to firing yourself first, we also need to do a bit of cartography, as we plan our journey to freedom. To help you plot your path, I've developed a tool to help you discern your personal why as well as create a road map for what to do next. This simple tool is called the End Game Clarity Map, and its overarching goal is to help you think through where you want to end up and what your final exit will be.

By completing the End Game Clarity Map, you look beyond your current business and contemplate your end game—where you want to finish. Then, you will work yourself backwards to start the process of firing yourself first. If you want a free downloadable version of the End Game Clarity Map, it's available on my website, www. FireYourselfFirst.com/resources.

Let's look at the four steps:

1. **Identify**: Identify where you are now. For this step, think about where you are today and describe your current situation. What have you created? What have you accomplished in the last ten years? What is working? What isn't working?

   This is the time to consider the difficulties you've faced. What challenges did you have to overcome to get to this point in your life? If you're like most people, I'm sure the road was not easy. Think back five, ten, and even twenty years ago. What were you like at those different points in your life? What about now? What changes occurred in you personally over the years? Did you survive the challenges that life threw your way? Are you a better person for having endured them?

2. **Contemplate:** After you've thought about your present, contemplate a future version of yourself. What does your ideal future look like? Where do you want to go? Think forward ten years from today. Where do you need to be ten years from now to feel happy about yourself? What accomplishments do you want to have completed? Do you want to be retired and living on a beautiful beach in Costa Rica? Would you prefer to be spending your days with family and grandchildren? Do you picture yourself on the golf course? What do you want your life to look like a decade from now?

3. **Clarify:** Now that you've imagined where you'd like to be in ten years, you might have gained a little insight into your personal why. Can you pinpoint what your personal why might be? Here are a few examples from the Why Institute:[7]

   o   To contribute to a great cause (to add value)
   o   To create relationships based on trust
   o   To make sense out of complex things
   o   To find a better way of doing things
   o   To do things the right way
   o   To challenge the status quo with a new way of thinking
   o   To seek mastery and understand

- o   To seek clarity
- o   To simplify

4. **Reflect:** Reflect on your obstacles, opportunities, and strengths. When it comes to obstacles, determine those you must eliminate now to have the future you desire. When it comes to opportunities, think about what opportunities you have and how you can leverage them to get where you want to be. What strengths do you bring to the table? Remember to take into consideration what you've done in the past to get you where you are today. If you've previously overcome your own personal Goliaths, then nothing can stop you from doing it again today. Finally, ask yourself whether you have any strengths you need to bring forward in your life.

Ultimately, the purpose of the End Game Clarity Map™ is to help you discern your personal why. Be sure to devote the time necessary to consider where you are and where you want to go.

Have a Plan: The 3-Step Planning Process

Now that you've taken the time to think about where you want to be in the future, it is time to start planning what you need to do to get there. That's where the plan comes into play–my 3-Step Planning Process to help you get from where you are to where you want to be. For instance, if you desire to sell your business, what steps do you need to take to do so? Or, if you want to keep your business because you love it and want it to generate cash, what steps do you need to take in this scenario? Here is where you need to be clear about what your fundamental aim is because your endgame will determine what steps you take.

1. Begin by thinking about your 3-year plan. What are three things you need to do in the next three years to secure the future you desire? Be sure to list no more than three action items per planning stage, so you don't overload yourself.
2. Think about your 1-year plan. What are three actions you need to take in the next year to establish your future?
3. What is your 90-day plan? What three things do you need to do in the next ninety days?
4. Finally, what's your 30-day plan? What are the top three actions you need to complete in the next thirty days?

As you plan, you'll begin to see the steps you need to take to fulfill all that you outlined in your End Game Clarity Map. Remember, we can't just aspire alone; we need to have a plan to reach them. So, take the time to plan out what you need to do in the coming days and years to live the life you've always dreamed of.

Other Tools to Discover Your Why

If you still need additional help to determine your personal why, Simon Sinek's book, *Start With Why,* and his workbook are excellent resources. Another tool you can use comes from the popular car company Toyota, and their method called the Five Whys, developed by Sakichi Toyoda, a Japanese inventor and industrialist. A quick Google search can provide more detail on this method, but in essence, you ask yourself a series of why questions to get to the root of a problem. Thus, the Five Whys is a simple and easy technique for solving problems when your primary goal is to find a problem's cause.

For example, you might start this method by asking yourself why you are interested in selling your company or setting it up as an ATM. When you do so, you might discover you want more time. Then, you might ask yourself why you want more time and discover that you've missed out on a lot of your family's life. If you continued to ask yourself a total of five whys, you might learn that you were so caught up in work that you put your family commitments last on the priority list, and you now feel compelled to give them their rightful place in your life. One of the beauties of the Five Whys is that by asking yourself why five times, you might discover that what you initially thought was the root of your problem turned out to be something completely different. The truth is, sometimes we aren't even sure of our genuine motives until we begin to ask ourselves why.

As you read the previous paragraph, perhaps some answers came to mind. Pause for a few moments and write down those responses.

1. Why? _____

_____

2. Why? _____

_____

3. Why? _____

_____

4. Why? _____

_____

5. Why? _____

_____

Moving Forward

So, why does all of this "personal why" stuff matter? Because, in the end, I don't simply want to free you from your business. My dream isn't to give you lots of time and money. My desire is for you to enjoy your life, to live a life well-lived, and to live the life you've always dreamed about living. However, if you don't know why you're doing what you're doing, if you haven't taken the time to consider what you enjoy, what makes you happy, and what fills your soul, then once you've unshackled yourself from your company, you're probably not going to enjoy your newfound freedom. Remember, firing yourself first is more than just a business decision—it's a personal one, a spiritual one—and so we must treat it as such.

By now, I hope you've done some work to help you discover your personal why. Perhaps you've implemented one or all the tools I provided. Maybe you've even asked a friend or a trusted mentor for help in the discovery process. Now, armed with the knowledge of *why* you are doing what you are doing and having taken the time to plan out *how* you are going to get there, you are now ready to move on to step 2— assembling a team who can run your company for you.

STEP 2

Hiring Your Autonomous Team (The 11-step Hiring Process)

To experience true independence, your team must work independently of you.

You've done the hard work of discovering your personal why, and it's time to move on to the second step in the Fire Yourself First Process—ensuring your team is ready to operate and grow without you! It doesn't matter whether you are planning to exit the business or set it up to run without you while you work on it a few hours a month. Either way, you need a trusted team in place who can run the company in your absence. That's what this chapter is all about—helping you evaluate your current team and helping you get rid of those not so valuable employees.

I love the book, *Who Not How: The Formula to Achieve Bigger Goals Through Accelerating Teamwork* by Dan Sullivan and Dr. Benjamin Hardy because they give you permission to let go of everything you do in your business that isn't fascinating and motivating to you. Dan and Ben go on to say

> It can be easy to focus on How, especially for high achievers who want to control what they can control, which is themselves. It takes vulnerability and trust to expand your efforts and build a winning team. It takes wisdom to recognize that 1) other people are more than capable enough to handle much of the Hows, and 2) that your efforts and contribution (your "Hows") should be focused exclusively where your greatest passion and impact are. Your attention and energy should not be spread thin, but purposefully directed where you can experience extreme flow and creativity.[8]

Remember, in order to grow, you first need to let go.

Evaluating (and Exiting) Your Own Responsibilities

The first step along the journey of evaluating your team is thinking about how *you* can exit your current responsibilities. Typically, we think we are the only person who can do what we do in our business. However, we must let go of that concept if we're going to be able to turn over our business operations. If you are planning on keeping your business and letting it run without you, then you need to start looking for someone who can fill a more senior role. This person will become your company's new president and will run the entire organization for you. Depending on how much or how little you want to continue to work, you could hire this person to be a COO, if you still desire to work a bit in the business, or a CEO if you want to work less. Cameron Herold is the founder of the COO Alliance, an organization where the world's COOs learn to be the best, and he sums up the COO role succinctly by saying:

> The COO's job is to make the CEO look good, to ensure all the pieces of the business are running as smoothly as possible and everyone in the organization is following its Vivid Vision® of the future.[9]

On the other hand, if your goal is to sell the business, then you will need, at the bare minimum, to have a president in place. This situation, though, has some challenges because, when it comes to potential buyers, different types of buyers have requirements they are looking for. For instance, if a buyer is looking to merge your company into theirs, then they may not need another president, and your business model with a president in place might not work for them. Other buyers, who want a self-running company with an excellent management team in place, are actually looking for a business that is fully operational and generating revenue on day one of the takeover. Regardless of who ends up purchasing your business, you must find a way to exit your current responsibilities. That step is crucial to ensuring your team can manage your company without you being present daily.

There's a paradox here I should mention. In step one, you thought about your personal why and what you really want from life. In doing so, you initiated a change in your relevance. As you release being relevant at work, you evolve to wanting to be more relevant in other spheres of life. To become more relevant in these other spaces, it is imperative that you become irrelevant in your business. Hence the paradox: to grow in relevance you must first become irrelevant to your company. But remember, relevance is not ending.

It's evolving.

In the end, the good news is that it's up to you as to how much you desire to be involved and it's also up to you as to how you will spend your newfound freedom. But first, you must set up the right people in the right roles, building a team that can provide you the flexibility you seek.

Evaluating The Process Chart

Whether you're selling or creating an ATM, now is the time to review and update your organizational chart, or what I prefer to call a process chart. Take a deep dive into your organization and identify all the processes, both big and small, necessary to create your product or offer your service. Upon review of your company's process chart, you'll find redundancies and missing processes. You might even discover certain processes lack an owner. Every process in your business must have one owner. As we all know, if more than one person is responsible for a process, then no one is responsible.

I can't overemphasize how important it is to identify all of your organization's processes. If you want to hand over your business to someone else to run, they must know *all* of the business operations. Everything must be clearly laid out to guarantee success.

Another important part of the chart is the hiring and firing processes. People (whether they be customers or team members) are complicated. In fact, there's nothing simple about dealing with the human race. As such, there are no tools, systems, or processes that will work for everyone, and along your entrepreneurial journey, you've gained a lot of insight into how people behave, both the good and the bad.

Have you taken the time to create processes that can ensure you're hiring the right fits for your organization while simultaneously getting rid of the wrong fits?

As a business owner, you know the costs involved with a miss in the hiring process, and these mis-hires cost us both time and money. Yet many organizations continue to repeat the same mistakes when it comes to hiring. As the famous quotation credited to Albert Einstein says:

> The definition of insanity is doing the same thing over and over again and expecting a different result.

Have you taken time to ensure you're not repeating hiring mistakes? What processes does your company have in place? Are these processes working?

Also, evaluate your goals for your business. Once you have clearly defined your personal goals using the End Game Clarity Map, you may want to use the same tool for your business. Where do you want to be in three years, one year, ninety days, or thirty days? Always be clear on what winning looks like for your business. If you want to go further, you may even want to create a Vivid Vision for your company. In his book, *Vivid Vision*, Cameron Herold says:

> A Vivid Vision is a detailed, three-to-four-page document that lays out a clear, logical vision of what your company will look like in three years. It's meant to be woven into your company's culture, guiding your employees' decision-making and giving all involved clear goals to strive for.[10]

Evaluating Your Current Team

As mentioned, the hiring process is critical, and as business owners, we must take the time to evaluate our teams. Do an inventory of every member and ask yourself a simple question:

Would I hire this person again?

The answer to this question must be a yes or a no. "Maybe" or "it depends" are not options. There are other questions to consider when thinking through who should be on your team. For example, you should ask yourself:

- Is this person ethical?
- Is this person trustworthy?
- Does this individual have the skills and ability to do the job?

If you have answered no to any of the previous questions, why is this person still working for you? I appreciate what author Patrick Lencioni wrote in his book, *The Ideal Team Player*. Lencioni says the three traits you should expect in high-performing team members are: Hungry, Humble, and (people) Smart.[11] I keep these traits in mind when interacting with team members. Do they have all three? You must critically evaluate each team member and ask yourself difficult questions. Afterward, the next step is simple. If you have identified team members who no longer seem like a good fit, create a plan to replace them.

Another part of the evaluation process is to consider any close family members employed by your business. If you plan to exit, this will affect family members working in the business. Now is the time for them also to begin the process of exiting the company. If a family member desires to remain, make it clear to the buyer where the person stands in the company. In addition, if you have family members in senior roles in the business, you must ensure they are competent in the eyes of *all* your current employees. Remember, all team members should be doing their jobs because they have the ability and the skills, not just because they are related to you. If the other team members don't believe your family members are capable, you will find it difficult to create a solid culture in the business.

When it comes to the company's culture, nothing is more important than hiring the right people, especially if you want a business that will run without you. Employees should be given a great place to work and come to work engaged. You must be relentless about removing people who don't fit your company's values and haven't bought into your purpose. The lack of the right people will destroy any hope you have of creating an autonomous business or one that will sell at its highest valuation. Remember, you are looking for a win-win relationship with your customers and suppliers, and you are also looking for a win-win with your employees.

Tips for Creating Your All-star Team

For over twenty years, I was the hiring guru. I read every book I could find on hiring and creating a solid work culture. During this time, part of my responsibility was to go to departments with problems and reorganize them. Over the years, I discovered sometimes I hired superstars, while other times I hired a dud. Luckily, most of my hires were winners. So, what happened with the duds?

Whenever I quickly hired an individual or based my decision on a "gut feeling," those were the times I ended up with a poor hire. I remember the last dud I hired. He threatened to sue me, and I had to pay him $10,000 to go away. For a business owner, the cost is great in terms of time, energy, and money when you hire a dud. According to the U.S. Department of Labor, the price of a bad hire is at least 30 percent of the employee's first-year earnings,[12] so for a $60,000/year employee that is $18,000! Who can afford to throw away $18,000?

After that unfortunate hiring experience, I vowed to become the best hiring expert I could be. I delved into even more books, talked to HR professionals, and tried to glean the best practices of those who hire the best team members. The truth is it's possible to get better at hiring people for our team. We only have to learn how.

Please note that I say team members—not employees. Some might wonder what difference it makes, but I assure you it does. As Strategic Coach and Entrepreneurial Team Strategist Shannon Waller notes, "A strong team is your best strategy for success."[13] The individuals you hire who connect with the business and with you are the best, most committed people. They also make the right decisions even when I am not present. Why? Because they are part of a team. They feel a connection and not like a cog in a big organization. Remember, people don't leave their jobs. They leave their managers.

Another thing to consider is salary. I always prefer to pay my employees over the going rate. Why? Because it enables me to hire a few people who are excellent, really type-A people. They are the people who will get the job done well. For example, I have one team member who does the work of three people. That's how good she is. As such, I don't mind paying her 20 percent over the local market rate. This individual is well worth her value. It's a win-win situation for both employer and employee to pay her well.

Be sure to think about the workplace culture. If you pay poorly and have a poor culture, you will lose people. As the business owner, the buck stops with you, and it is your responsibility to create an environment that fosters culture, vision, and accountability.

> **As the business owner, the buck stops with you, and it is your responsibility to create an environment that fosters culture, vision, and accountability.**

When I speak of culture, I don't mean having pinball machines and sleep pods for the team to use. That's not real culture. I'm talking about creating what Howard Schultz, the founder of Starbucks, calls "The Third Place." This is a place where people want to go, where they feel valued, and, not surprisingly, where they give 110 percent. This is also a place where you're going to have a team who can run your company for you and enable you to fire yourself first.

Finally, hire positive people. Positive people attract other positive people, both in other team members and with customers. I've also found it works the other way: negative people attract negative people and clients. So, make sure to hire positive, upbeat people. In doing so, you will create a positive environment for team members and customers.

Solving the Hiring Crisis

So, how do we hire the right people, the superstars we love, while avoiding the duds? Who are those "A players," who come to work fully charged and excited? They're the people who don't need you to motivate them because they naturally love executing and doing the best job they can. They are the people we long to hire because they need only high-level guidance to execute and do their jobs. They do their jobs well, and they do it with a great frame of mind. These are the true all-stars. Unfortunately, regardless of what is happening in the economy, these winners can be difficult to find. It seems only about one out of ten potential team members are the winners. If that's the case, how do we find them?

I needed a repeatable process that allowed me to hire the best people because I understood that having a great team would let me scale my company quickly. Time is the most valuable commodity, and wasting six to nine months in hiring, firing, and then hiring another person wasn't a viable option. I had to hire the right person from the start. So, to find the superstars and avoid the duds, I created an 11-step hiring process. Thankfully, it doesn't matter if you are in an employee's or employer's market—this process will work for you.

This 11-step process is what I follow, and I now get very consistent hiring results. However, discovering the right way to hire didn't happen overnight. It took time to understand what I was looking for and trying to avoid. Over the last twenty years, I've hired both winners and losers, and the entire time, I thought I was using the same process in hiring.

But I was wrong.

I wasn't using a process at all. It's no wonder I had the occasional bad hire. That changed once I implemented my 11-Step Hiring Process™.

The 11-Step Hiring Process

From the start, let me warn you: don't ignore any of these steps. While I understand that eleven steps might seem like a lot, I'm telling you—if you ignore even one of them, it will cost you both time and money. How do I know? Every time I have ignored a step to speed up the hiring process, it has cost me. As you begin to use this new hiring process, it may feel difficult or even uncomfortable. This is normal as the process is brand-new. However, soon you will be able to do these eleven steps in your sleep, and you will save thousands of dollars by putting in the time to hire correctly and avoid those unfortunate duds.

The genesis of these eleven steps came about unexpectedly. One of my businesses was a cosmetic medical clinic, and when I posted a job opening for a nurse, I would receive over two hundred applications. I didn't have the time to quickly review all two hundred applications, let alone thoroughly examine the applicants. (My goal with this business was to work no more than a couple of hours per month.) While it's possible to have an administrative assistant preview all of the applicants, I am more interested in having an automated, quick, and reliable process rather than taking someone's time away from the other tasks at hand. For every applicant, I apply all eleven steps until they fail one. If they fail at any particular point, I end the hiring process with a quick, "Thank you for applying. We will keep you in mind" email.

When it comes to your business, do not underestimate the importance of your team. Whether you plan to sell the company or scale back your time, you need an effective team in place. Having the best team is one of the keys to enable you to fire yourself first. My 11-step hiring process will help you get there.

You or your hiring department can follow these steps. Feel free to download the 11-step hiring guide at www. FireYourselfFirst.com/resources.

Step 1: The Job Application

Before you begin the hiring process, create an online application. I use online form software (Google Forms, Wufoo, etc.), or you can utilize online job posting software with a job-posting questions template. You can also create your customized job form. Once my company has the application, we post it on our website in the career section so potential team members can read about the job description and expectations. We list the job overview, roles, responsibilities, and requirements. While this process is meant to be a win-hire for you, you also need it to be a win for the employee. You don't want to spend three to six months training someone only to learn the person isn't a good fit and doesn't enjoy working at your company. Take your time upfront. I'm sure you've heard the phrase, "Hire slowly, fire fast!" That is what you are doing here. You are taking your time to find the winners—don't be in a hurry.

We also have a short form for applicants to complete, and I keep this form to three to five questions. Begin by asking a few simple questions and follow up with questions that require more in-depth answers. When designing the questions, think about the traits required for the position and consider how to discover that information. For example, if I'm going to hire a nurse to document patient charts and make notes of every patient interaction as part of the job, then having a detail-oriented person is extremely important. Otherwise, you could run into liability issues.

It's important that the nurse's handwriting doesn't look like chicken scratch, and also that the notes are clear, specific, and highly detailed. Therefore, in the form, I'll ask a specific, detail-oriented request of the applicant such as, "Please address the cover letter to Jeff Russell." When I implemented that one specific, detailed request, two hundred applicants dropped to sixty! It's more manageable to handle sixty applications as opposed to over two hundred. If applicants can't follow a simple instruction, then you don't want them working in a detail-oriented position. They wouldn't be a good fit, and a simple question highlighted those better suited for the position.

While the cover letter request was geared for those seeking a nurse's position, it's easy to apply the concept to other positions. For instance, how important is being detail-oriented for the chief financial officer of your business? Or an executive assistant? To have someone in charge of your accounts receivable, you need someone accountable and detail-oriented because the person will be responsible for all those numbers and ensuring the business's credits and debits are correct. What about a team member who will be emailing customers? This person must have good grammar and communicate clearly. Consider each team member's position and tailor your application according to the specific needs of the position. Doing so will attract superstars and help you to avoid duds.

This step is imperative because there are lazy people out there, and most applicants are just looking for another j-o-b where they can do the least and get paid the most. For the employer, this is not a win-win situation, but a win-lose. The employee wins by garnering the most money for the least amount of work, but the owner loses. By hiring the right people, the superstars, we can *all* win.

Another question I ask is, "What have you done in the last year to improve your knowledge?" Times are changing more than they've ever changed in the history of the world. You may have been able to go from 1970 to 1980 and experience little change, but that is no longer the case. Questions pop up all the time such as:

Does your company take Apple Pay®?
What about Google Pay®?
Ethereum?
Bitcoin?

This is all in addition to the standard Visa® and MasterCard®.

How does this relate to the hiring process? It's

It's a red flag when a person hasn't improved their knowledge in an ever-changing world.

a red flag when a person hasn't improved their knowledge in an ever-changing world. If they haven't done anything to improve then they are not a right fit. For instance, my medical business is changing all the time. My training business is also changing, even the software we use. The software we use today didn't even exist three years ago. I need team players who can learn new information quickly. If they can't, that's a problem. That's why asking a simple question is so powerful—it reveals whether the individual possesses a growth mindset as opposed to a limited mindset. It also reveals if they want to do the least possible amount of work, which translates into how they will work in your business.

Ask where they currently work, since the best candidates are typically employed. Ask whether they have experience with some of the services you offer or have the skills required. Understand how they solve problems so ask a question such as, "What are your go-to sources of information when you don't know something?" I am hoping they respond with mentors, online tools, associations, training websites, then co-workers, and so on. This is an important question because team members need to troubleshoot on his or her own.

Understand what their big goals are. Ask questions such as, "Tell me about your dream job and be as detailed as possible." See whether they want to move up or start their own business. If they are looking to start their own business, this might be a concern. They may be here only to learn and then leave. These candidates aren't what you're looking for because you want long-term team members.

Ultimately, the purpose of this first step is to weed out lazy people and pre-qualify potential candidates. Gauge their ability to follow detailed instructions, examine their grammar, determine how they work and how they find things out they don't know. Learn whether they have the necessary skills and what they want in life. Depending on the role, ask them to include their LinkedIn profile, as this is a more professional network than Facebook.

Step 2: Resume and Cover Letter Review

As mentioned earlier, for the cover letter, I like to add something such as, "Please address your cover letter to Jeff Russell, Practice Manager," to check if they can follow simple directions. Another thing to examine in their cover letter is how well they write because, with many of the roles in business, they will be required to write thank-you notes or emails. So, correct grammatical usage is important. Use the resume to quickly examine the list of the applicant's skills and how long they worked at each previous business. If they haven't spent more than a year at any of their previous jobs, then it's unlikely yours will be any different. The truth is, leaving employers quickly is a sign of a bad employee. While it is possible the person likes to move around searching for a challenge, this indicates a lack of traits you want in long-term team members.

In step 2, focus on where the applicant has previously worked and if they are working now, which signifies an A-Player. If they are not working, why is that? Note if they have previously worked in a job similar to the one they are applying for. As the employer, ask yourself if the applicant can grow with your business. Getting a good resume and cover letter is a crucial part of finding your great hires. You can also use them as a basis for asking questions in future interviews.

Step 3: Email Questions

If a person has managed to get this far in the process, the next step is to send an email. This individual will likely communicate with customers and the other people within the organization. So, make sure the person communicates well. Ensure their language is mature and professional, as opposed to teen-aged texts. Your customers will receive communications from this individual, so they must be up for the task in every capacity—including language use. The email is a good check of an applicant's language skills and grammar.

It's your job, as the owner, to ensure all your employees can communicate well with everyone involved in your company. Your employees are a part of your brand, and you need to hire them as such.

This email includes two or three questions. For example, why are they leaving their current position? This simple question provides valuable information and their personality a little more. For example, are they leaving their current company because work has slowed down? Great—that shows they're a go-getter. Are they leaving because they are bored? Wonderful—they want a challenge. Look for someone who wants to leave so they can grow. However, are they leaving because there's a personality conflict with their current boss and/or coworkers? Are they looking for more money? Be aware that some responses could be red flags, so use your discernment.

This step is the beginning of the interview process. Most people don't have time to meet with every applicant in person and only want to do so if the applicant appears strong. By posing two or three pre-interview questions in this email, you can evaluate how they answer and determine whether they should move on to the next step.

Some other questions to ask:

- **What do you like doing the most at your current job?** Don't go right to the "money" questions. This question is an easy buffer. Hopefully, the answer includes something required for the position they are applying for.

- **Are you currently paid salary, salary and commission, or only commission?** Depending on the answer, you might ask in the next email or interview step how their pay was structured. Their answer may provide ideas on how to make improvements to your compensation program, and it also helps reveal their expectations.

- ***What is your salary range?*** Make sure they are in your range. If they don't answer, unless you are desperate, end the hiring process here.

One final tip: note how quickly they respond to your email questions. Determine if their answers seem relevant and well thought out. You're looking for the A-Players.

Step 4: The 30-minute Phone Interview

The next step in the hiring process is the phone call, but only after:

- Checking their cover letter and resume
- Reviewing their online social media presence
- Looking at photos to ensure they are congruent with the organization's culture
- Determining they've passed the email test

If the applicant has made it this far, then conduct a phone or Zoom call lasting from five to thirty minutes.

When it comes to Zoom, prepare to see an individual in their residence, which most likely isn't set up for a business. Don't expect an amazing background or for the audio and video to be perfect. Those aren't fair expectations for the applicant or even yourself.

So, what should you look for in a Zoom interview?

1. See whether they bothered to get out of their pajamas.
2. Check their mannerisms. Listen to their voice and how they speak.

Sometimes, it helps to do a second Zoom call or another phone call, especially if you're interviewing for a more senior role in the company.

Step 4 takes time but it's much more efficient to talk with potential hires on the phone rather than meeting in person. The purpose of the phone interview is to pre-qualify them for an in-person interview. In this step, find out why they applied and what motivates them. Ask a question such as, "What do you want to be doing in five to ten years?" The only purpose of the phone interview is to find out whether the applicant should move to an in-person interview.

During a phone or in-person interview, ask open-ended questions. Then stay quiet and let the applicant answer. Your main job here is to listen—not to talk. You can't learn much if you're talking. Listening is a key skill for most things in life and especially during the interview process. While listening, look for recent and relevant information. If they give vague answers, request specifics. Ask, "Tell me more about that situation."

The candidate needs to be a quick learner. Because technology evolves so quickly, you'll train them with what you currently use in business, but they'll also need to learn software, procedures, and other technologies not available yet. Listen for examples of when they had to learn something quickly.

*   How did they find the experience?

- Was it stressful?
- Did they find it challenging yet fun?

Here are some other questions to ask:

- *"Why did you apply?"* Are they looking for a *j-o-b*? If they are, that is not who you are looking for. Look for someone who is already working yet wanting a role where they can expand their knowledge and, above all, where they can help customers.

- *"What do you know about our business?"* If they haven't taken the time to review your website and find out what you do, don't hire them.

- *"Tell me about your ideal job?"* Gauge their expectations of an ideal job and determine whether that is something you can provide. If they are looking to move up the ladder, that could be a problem in a small company where the opportunity for growth is limited. The ideal response is, "A positive work environment that is drama-free and a role where I can help people."

- *"How would you describe a motivational work environment?"* The candidate will typically tell you what they are not getting. Their answers are important because they will tell you about their expectations. For example, if they want daily acknowledgment of a job well done, can you give them that? If you are not a natural cheerleader who is always saying, "Great work," then this person may find your work environment demotivating. If they say they want a gossip- and drama-free work environment, you had better not allow gossip to fester in your business.

- *"When I call your past supervisors, how would they rate you on a scale of 1 to 10?"* Be clear that you will call their previous supervisors. This prompts them to answer more honestly. You can follow up with the open-ended question: "Why?" This question encourages them to open up about what they do well.

Other items to take into consideration are:

- Are they positive?
- Are they organized?
- Do they have the required skills?
- Do they know what they want to do?
- Did they send a thank-you email?

You may also want to go review their resume and verify or clarify some of their experience. Ask why they left each job, which helps spot trends.

- Did they change jobs because they were always trying to move up?
- Was there always a problem with their boss? If there was, you can be sure they will have a problem with you!

Step 5: The Technical Test

If everything is going well, ask the applicant to do something. See if they can do the job required. Give them a little test or activity that is relevant to the position but doesn't require much time. Plus, any individual who doesn't want to give a result will not be hired. If they are interested in being a marketing manager, ask them to send an example of a strategic marketing plan they have created. If they refuse to do so, they are out of the application process. If they ask for money to fulfill the task, they also fail.

Here are a few examples of technical tests to give to a potential hire. It needs to be a short test of something they would be required to do in their job.

- For someone working directly with customers, ask them to send an example of an online review request email they would send to a customer after a purchase.
- For a receptionist, ask for some example phone scripts to use when answering the phone in different situations, such as dealing with an angry customer, a new customer, someone asking for directions, and so on.

In this fifth step, determine whether they want the job. If they can't do a simple twenty-minute task, they are not the right person. If they ask for money, they are not the right person. This is where the candidate might realize this role isn't the right one. The goal is to weed out lazy people only looking for a paycheck. The A-players love an established process and the many steps involved in the hiring process because they are interviewing you too!.

Step 6: The In-person Interview

As the owner, you must protect your time. So, the in-person interview doesn't happen until the sixth step in the hiring process. You may only interview the candidates who will report directly to you and have your hiring team interview all other candidates. If you are not comfortable doing interviews, you may want to interview everyone at first to get comfortable. The other option is to have the candidates interviewed by someone you know with interviewing experience. At this stage in the game, you need to pay attention to how the individual handles questions. Consider whether they *light up* when you talk to them.

In this step, only talk to the leading candidates. Someone can be very different in person, so this is critical. I've had applicants successfully go through the first five steps only to have the hiring process come to a complete halt when I met them in person.

This is not the time to give people a pass.

Make sure they stand out and are a good fit with the current members of your team. Learn whether you and other team members can work with this individual and whether your clients will like this person.

This is also time to evaluate their appearance. Make sure they are a cultural fit for your business. For example, if you are hiring a receptionist for a high-ticket consulting business, professional business attire is important. For someone working the loading dock or in a creative role, wearing professional business attire doesn't matter as much. With any customer-facing roles, you want them to dress similarly to your customer, whether golf attire or a suit and tie. Take into consideration your business and the overall culture. What is significant when it comes to appearances for your particular company?

The goal of the in-person interview is to see how well the applicant prepared for the interview process. Your gut reaction will give you that answer within 30-60 seconds of meeting them. Consider the role they are applying for and their need to fit that role. At this point, you may not feel satisfied with how they answered questions during the phone interview, so ask additional questions to get a better understanding.

Here are some questions to ask during the in-person interview:

- *"Tell me about yourself."* Learn what the person likes to do during their time. Do they go for walks? Play golf? Read? Cook? Workout? Make sure this person has a life outside of work. You may find some activities that can benefit your business.

- *"What are you looking for in your next job? What is important to you?"* Look for tips on what they don't like about their current and/or past jobs. You may uncover some warning signs of behavior that is most likely to continue after you hire them. For example, If they hate to be micromanaged, you better not be a micromanager!

- *"What would your current/past supervisor say your strongest point is? What would your current/past supervisor say your weakest attribute is?"* Both are textbook questions, but the purpose is to see how self-aware they are. Most people are more critical of themselves than others. See how humble they are or, on the flip side, how arrogant. If they answer, "I'm a perfectionist," ask for an example where being a perfectionist caused unnecessary drama in their workplace. They are not usually ready for that one!

- *"Who was your best boss and who was the worst?"* This question gives insight into their expectations of the organization's leadership. You know your culture, so your job is to assess whether your company can meet their expectations. If not, this person will likely become discouraged and quit, causing you to repeat the hiring procedure.

- *"Tell me about a time you had a conflict at work with a coworker?"* In many businesses, work is done in teams. This can be a recipe for disaster and drama, so new hires must have conflict-resolution skills. Otherwise, you can be assured drama will result. Look for people who are aware of dramatic situations and proactively try to solve them. Don't hire the person who always expects their supervisor to solve their problems. This shows a lack of accountability and ability to problem solve.

- *"Have you ever worked in a situation where the rules and guidelines were not clear? Tell me about it. How did you feel about it? How did you react?"* The fact is, this is going to happen, especially if you are not there on a day-to-day basis. You want team members who will follow your standard operating procedures and are confident enough to make decisions when you are not present.

- *"Describe a situation in which you effectively* **read** *another person and based your actions on their needs and values."* This is a key to any role in business. Everyone must have an awareness of what others are thinking and feeling. It's especially important when working with clients since you should be able to read if the client feels understood. Your team should also be able to identify whether the client is happy with the product or service offered. Your goal is to create a legion of happy clients who will go on and tell their friends about your business. If you can't tell if someone is pleased with the product or service, you have a problem!

- *"Tell us about a time when you used facts and reason to persuade someone to accept your recommendation."* This is a good question for someone working with customers. The candidate needs to know how to educate and recommend the products and services that fit your customers.

- *"Give a specific example of when you had to address an angry customer. What was the problem and what was the outcome? How would you assess your role in diffusing the situation?"* Not everyone will be a happy customer, so everyone in the company must have great conflict management skills. Their answer will show whether they have the skills to handle those rare, unhappy clients.

- *"Describe a situation when you demonstrated initiative and took action without waiting for direction. What was the outcome?"* Many people find satisfaction working in an environment where what they do matters, and often the best ideas come from those working directly with customers. You don't want to hire robots that work with the customers and send them on their way. You want observant people who recommend improvements for both the business's and customers' satisfaction.

- *"Tell me about a time when you had to work under pressure."* Here you will find out how they handle stress, which will occur in an autonomous business.

Ask other questions about specific skills needed for the job. The person doesn't need to have all of the skills, but they should be able to show a strong aptitude to learn. You may want to see what their experience is with any software your business uses (word processing, spreadsheets, customer database, e-newsletters, etc.) and social media software (Facebook, Instagram, TikTok, Twitter, etc.). It's always favorable to learn you have a software superstar on your team, because the rate of technology change isn't going to slow down any time soon!

These two questions signal the end of the interview:

- *"What hours are you available? When are you available?"* It's nice to know whether they need to give two weeks' notice at their current employer and want to take a week off for a vacation.

- *"Do you have any questions for me?"* If they don't have any questions, that could be a bad sign. Typically, the best candidates always have a question or two. If you get an insightful question such as, "What are the business's three-year goals?" you may have a winner. They are looking into the future, both yours and theirs. When a candidate asks a question or two, it's a sign they are interested in you and working for the business. If they don't ask any questions, they could simply be looking for any *j-o-b*. Potentially the person is just nervous.

Step 7: In-person Interview with Current Team Members

If an applicant passes the in-person interview, have them meet with other team members without you. Here you are doing a gut check with your other team members. Can they work with this person? How does the applicant interact with the team in your absence?

Your team needs to be part of the hiring process. If not, they may not embrace the new hire. If you have a drama-free team in place, they will want to keep it that way and will help you weed out any troublemakers.

In addition, your team must not wing it. Give your team structure by providing the following *cultural fit* questions to ask the applicant:

- *"What was it like working at your last (current) company?"* Is the candidate a complainer, or do they focus on the positive? Do they smile when they talk about positive things? If not, they may not be forthright in their answers. If they list how bad things were there (even though they may have been), they are more likely a negative person and not a good fit. If they spend time talking about the culture of their current or previous role, you know that culture is important to them.

- *"What could your last (current) company have done better?"* This is a follow-up to the previous question. Do they have any ideas about improvements? You are looking for someone who wants to improve. Have they taken the time to think about problems and come up with solutions, or do they dwell on problems and expect management to come up with the solutions? Are they a team player and solutions-oriented?

- *"What did you like least about your last position?"* This is a double-check question to make sure they don't hate what they will do in this new role. If they hate doing a part of the job that is a key part of their role, you have a problem!

- *"Describe what the ideal work environment looks like to you?"* Find out if they are going to enjoy your business's culture and workflow. Do they like a lot of structure? Do they like doing different things throughout the day or prefer repetitive tasks? Does their preference match the role in your business?

- *"How do you rely on others to make you better?"* This is a team player and self-awareness question to determine whether they see the importance and benefits of working in a team. They should know they don't know everything, and it's okay to rely on fellow team members to learn and grow.

- *"When working on a team, what role do you like to play?"* There are several roles on a team: leader, investigator, scribe, contributor, coordinator, and implementer. Find out what they like to do and see if it conflicts with other team members.

- *"How do you like to recharge your batteries?"* This is a great question, especially when the team will work closely together. Some people need to recharge their batteries by leaving the business at lunch or taking a couple of 15-minute breaks outside every day. Everyone needs space to recharge.

- *"What does teamwork mean to you?"* Their answer demonstrates how they interpret teamwork. If the candidate says everybody figures out a solution on their own and then reports back to the team, that's good to know, especially if your culture values team brainstorming for problem-solving.

- *"What do you do if you have a conflict with another team member?"* Are your existing team members comfortable with their style of conflict resolution?

- *"What is the one thing you must have in your work environment for you to know that this is the right role for you?"* Hopefully, this is something your culture provides!

You might also want to throw in some role-specific questions:

- *"What is your experience doing _____?"* See if they have the experience needed for the job.

- *"If a customer says they can only come in at 4 pm Thursday and you are only working until 3 pm, what do you do?"* You'll determine the candidate's willingness to go above and beyond the call of duty.

- *"Do you have any problem working the occasional evening or Saturday?"* If the question is relevant, it will help show if they have any home issues that might impact working late and/or on weekends.

After the team interview, follow up with your team. Is the candidate someone they can work with? Sometimes, you may love this person, but your team says they are not the right fit. If that happens, you will need to decide. I have found out the hard way that it's best to side with your team and not hire that candidate!

After the team interview, phone the candidate for their perception of the interview and ask if they have any follow-up questions. Use the call for any additional questions you or your team have.

Step 8: The Reference Check

The importance of a reference check cannot be overstated, as past behavior is an indicator of future behavior. But this can be difficult. Someone's resume could show they've been with the same company for the last eight years, which means their most recent reference could be eight years old! A lot can happen in eight years! Some references may not even work there anymore. Make sure you do a reference check–whenever I didn't, I paid for it!

Make sure you do a reference check–whenever I didn't, I paid for it!

This step may be uncomfortable for many people, but it is a critical part of the hiring process. On the positive side, the calls usually take only 10-15 minutes.

It's helpful to think outside of the box when checking references. I once hired a marketing manager, and at that time, I only had a 3-step hiring process. This individual worked for a large, well-known legal firm during the last five years, so I assumed she wouldn't be a dud. Because calling the legal firm for a reference check could cause her to lose her job (and potentially open me up to a lawsuit), I decided to forego it. What could go wrong? I thought, so I hired her.

Big mistake.

On the first day of work, she arrived half an hour late. She called me to explain that she had just witnessed an accident and needed to wait for the police to give a statement. She assured me she should be at work in about twenty minutes. While the scenario sounded strange, I recognized it could happen, so I gave her the benefit of the doubt.

On her second day of work, I received yet another call. "I'm so sorry. I'm going to be late. My tire blew, and I'm just waiting for AAA to show up. I'll be there as soon as they have it fixed." What are the chances of two odd things happening two days in a row? While I recognized this was a bit strange, I also thought, "Hey, it can happen."

Until the third day of work.

Can you guess what happened on her third day? I received another call with a new excuse: "My sister is in the hospital, and she's having her baby early. I won't be able to make it in until this afternoon." At this point, my Spidey senses tingled, and I knew there was no way this was all a coincidence.

While the situation did improve after that third day, she was always late. However, the real problem was that I had hired her to be a marketing manager and she didn't possess the ability to do the job. Her lack of technical know-how confused me. She has been the marketing manager of a prestigious law firm for the past five years. What was going on?

I learned a new, secret step to add to the hiring process— verify current employment.

Because her employment had been dicey from the start, I searched for her law firm on LinkedIn. I found the name of her supervisor and called. Since she worked for me, I had no reason *not* to call and ask for a reference check. The supervisor revealed my new marketing manager had a penchant for tardiness and had been fired six months ago. She wasn't even working at the law firm when she applied for my job opening. I caught her in lie number one!

The tale didn't stop there.

I continued the off-the-record conversation with the supervisor and discovered that many of the lies my current employee had used on me—the accident, the flat tire, and so on—had been used on her previous employer as well. I had hired a liar and a dud but was determined not to do this again.

For every person you bring in for an interview, do a bit of an investigation before the meeting:

1. Check out their LinkedIn and Facebook social media profiles because they usually show current employment.
2. Call the company and ask to speak to the applicant on the phone. This verifies they are still working there.

The fact is, the wrong-fit employees are pretty obvious to spot, but liars are the toughest to identify. Implement this extra step to ensure you don't get stuck with a dud or worse, a lying dud.

Liars can easily manipulate the hiring process, they are the ones who are the most difficult to fire, and they cause the most damage along the way. Dave Ramsey of Ramsey Solutions calls these people donkeys. As Ramsey says, you don't want a donkey working in the stable. A resume isn't all that helpful in the hiring process because people will claim they are still working for their past employer, even after they were fired. What causes them to have such bravado? They know you're not going to take the time to call and check on a reference.

Always, always do a reference check and verify current employment.

Taking the time to hire the best people is paramount because the largest expense for any business is payroll. Allocate sufficient time to get the best return on your financial investment. If you are going to have an autonomous business, you must have a trusted team in place who can operate your company on your behalf. Ask yourself, can my team run this business without me? If so, congratulations! If not, get to work on your hiring process.

Here are the steps in a reference check:

1. Ask the candidate for a list of references from current supervisors or business owners. If the candidate doesn't provide a list of references, this is a red flag. They should have done such a good job that they would be happy to give you references and contact information.

2. If you receive a list of former supervisors that usually means the references are friends so ignore them. Instead, check LinkedIn or the company's "About Us" section to find out who is in charge. If the company is large, try to find the candidate's supervisor. If it is smaller, call the owner directly.

3. You want to have at least two references, and their answers should be consistent. Ideally, you want to talk to four or five references—the more the better.

4. Keep the reference call short. Don't waste this person's time.

5. Have your questions prepared.

The first question is the most important: "Would you rehire this person?"

The answer you want is, "Yes!" A long pause is a red flag. If they give you a cautious yes with parameters (i.e., "If we had a position that was suitable"), then you need to learn more. Hearing this question first often throws the reference off guard and they answer from their gut, which is what you want.

If they answer positively, ask the following questions to get a better idea of how the person likes to be managed. If you don't manage your employees the way they like to be managed, they may not be a good fit for your business.

Here are some follow-up questions:

- *"How long was _____ employed in your firm?"* Make sure this matches what they have on their resume.

- *"Can you tell me why _____ left?"* It should be the same story you heard from the candidate.

- *"What was it like to supervise _____?"* You want to get some insight into what kind of person they were as an employee.

- *"Do you have any tips or suggestions on how to best motivate and guide _____?"* You can often get great tips here on how to manage and motivate them.

- *"What were their strengths?"* Does this match what they said in the interview? This answer shows whether the candidate is self-aware.

- *"Was there one thing that stands out as a noteworthy accomplishment in their job?"* This is an optional question, but you may get an example of when the employee went above and beyond.

- *"Where did you feel _____ needed to improve their skills to do their job more effectively?"* This is an important question and should match what the candidate said were their "weaknesses" during the interview.

- *"How much interest did they show in learning/development in their job?"* New procedures will be added, and technology is always changing. Do they embrace or resist change?

- *"Did _____ demonstrate willingness and ability to put in additional or long hours?"* Looking for that natural trait to go above and beyond and someone who is not just looking for another j-o-b.

- *"Is there anything else you would like to add or advice you would like to share?"* References will often give their summary of the employee, and you may hear more tips on how to manage and motivate the candidate.

The goal of the reference check is two-pronged:

1. Did the employee leave on good terms? Are they good team members? Remember, history often predicts future behavior.
2. Learn how they like to be managed and consider whether you have a culture that fosters that outcome.

You should be able to talk to two or three references within thirty minutes. You might feel uncomfortable at first, but by using the above questions as a guide, the reference check should be quick and insightful. To help get you more comfortable, call up a friend and practice the questions. If you skip this part of the hiring process, it will cost you. As Nike® says, "Just Do It!"

Step 9: DiSC® Personality Assessment

After a successful reference check, learn more about how the person thinks and processes information and about their communication preferences. You want as few surprises as possible. The DiSC Personality test (www.discprofile.com) can help you understand how someone works, thinks and likes to receive feedback. Others like to use a more inexpensive tool like Gallup's CliftonStrengths®.[14] Some people like to use these tools earlier in the hiring process, but I don't. Without performing a comprehensive interview and reference check, knowing the online test results in advance can skew your bias toward them. For instance, most people have a natural bias to hire people like them. Depending on the position you are hiring for and your existing team, this may be a good idea or may cause you many headaches. Hire for your team's deficiencies because it's key to a winning team and successful business.

What is the DiSC profile? It is a system that breaks down personality types into four categories: D-I-S-C. Every person is a mixture of all four personality traits, with one being more dominant. Here is a summary of the four profiles of the DiSC system. The individual reports sent after the test provide more in-depth information about you and your team.

DiSC Personality Types:

- **D** (Decisive): This person is a hard-charging driver who isn't too concerned about how their decisions will affect others' feelings. They want to get the job done—and get it done quickly.
- **I** (Interactive): This personality style is a party waiting for a place to happen. They are loaded with energy and love being around people.
- **S** (Stabilizing): The S personality is amiable, loyal, anti-conflict, and concerned about pace. They can be slow in making decisions, but only because they want everyone onboard.
- **C** (Cautious): The C is the rule keeper—analytical, factual, and obsessed with detail and procedures. They can seem rigid, but to them, the rules are the rules, and there is a reason for each one.

STYLE	WANTS	NEEDS
D (Decisive)	To achieve	Responsibility
I (Interactive)	To be included	Recognition
S (Stabilizing)	To contribute	Appreciation
C (Cautious)	To create efficiency	Affirmation

This assessment is a powerful tool to help you find the right hire for your business. For example, if the position requires confidence, then it's critical you hire someone who is a high "D" (decisive) and/or "I" (Interactive). What you don't want is too high with a "C" (cautious) or "S" (stabilizing). If someone is lower on one of the personalities than you would like, do you still hire them? For the most part, if you are aware of their weaknesses, you can work on the individual with a combination of understanding from you and additional training.

If you still have concerns based on their profile results, have a quick phone conversation. If the person has a very low "D" (decisive) score, you may have them give you some examples of when they have been decisive (i.e., "What do you do when you have multiple tasks and things start spinning out of control?"). After this follow-up phone call, if you are still not happy with the responses, the applicant is not the best person for the role.

Kolbe™ Assessment

Another test I like to incorporate into the hiring process is the Kolbe assessment. Kolbe Indexes help you understand how people naturally approach tasks and work. It's not a personality test, and it doesn't tell you how smart you are. You get immediately actionable advice to grow a team and be more productive with less pain. After working with the Kolbe System™, you'll be able to empower people to be at their best when you need them the most.[15]

Kolbe Indexes are based on conation — the part of the mind that governs how you actually get things done when striving. Think of it as your instinctive strengths.

Your conative attributes define the way you take action and your approach to productivity. Understand your unique attributes as strengths and leverage them to do more, more naturally, in every aspect of your daily life.

Your Kolbe result will describe your natural strengths – your modus operandi (MO).

Kolbe's four Action Modes are the modern breakthrough in understanding and explaining conation. Kathy

Kolbe's key insight was that everyone has a strength in how they operate in each of these Action Modes. Each person's method of operation, or "MO," is their strength in that area.

FACT FINDER

The instinctive need to probe and the way we gather and share information. Behavior ranges from gathering detailed information and documenting strategies to simplifying and clarifying options. This Action Mode deals with detail and complexity, providing the perspective of the past.

FOLLOW THRU

The instinctive need to pattern and the way we organize and design. Behavior ranges from being systematic and structured to being adaptable and flexible. This Action Mode deals with structure and order and provides focus and continuity.

QUICK START

The instinctive need to improvise and the way we deal with risk and uncertainty. Behavior ranges from driving change and innovation to stabilizing and preventing chaos. This Action Mode deals with originality and risk-taking and provides intuition and a sense of vision.

IMPLEMENTOR

The instinctive need to demonstrate and the way we handle space and tangibles. Behavior ranges from making things more concrete by building solutions to being more abstract by imagining a solution. This Action Mode deals with physical space and provides durability and a sense of the tangible.

Knowing your employees' (and family members') Kolbe Index Score allows you to see how they will function in the "wild," without supervision. Every role in your organization will have a different preferred Kolbe score. For example, if you have an executive assistant, you'll want them to have very high follow through and fact finder scores. A sales role is better suited for someone with a higher quick start and lower fact finder score. If you are going to implement Kolbe, it's best to have someone on your team become certified on their system.

Step 10: The Lunch Interview with Owner and Team Members (This is optional, depending on the level of employment.)

As you near the end of the hiring process, have a team meeting with the prospective employee over lunch and assess how the applicant interacts with key team members. It's good to see how the applicant and your team interact in a more casual environment. People are more nervous when they meet you at your company, but they relax at a restaurant. Be sure not to pick an expensive restaurant. Something casual will help the person relax. This step doesn't apply to every potential employee but is only for a key role.

This lunch interview will also allow you and other team members to ask questions that arose after the earlier interview and/or the DiSC profile results.

Step 11: The 90-day Probation

The final step is a probationary period with the new hire. Write into their employment contract that you can fire this person during the probationary period for any reason, and similarly, they can leave the company for any reason. Because they are signing a legal contract, they will pause and consider whether this is the right job.

Even though some states are "at-will" employment states, meaning you can fire someone at any time for any reason without recourse, it's wise to put everyone on a 90-day probationary period. This forces you to pay attention to how they work, how they interact with other team members, what their manner is with customers, and whether you like them or not.

If you and/or your team members find the new hire to have excellent skills, but they annoy everyone on the team, get rid of them!

Trust me. The situation will not improve. Each person has a specific personality, and if it hasn't changed by now, it's unlikely to change. If you are not in an "at will" state, you have only 90 days to let a person go without cause. In this final step of the hiring process, you assess their work ethic, communication skills, and cultural fit.

What is the end goal of this extensive hiring process? Creating your autonomous team, that wonderful group of people who will run your company and free you up for the life you've always dreamed of living.

While it will take time to implement every step, it will be worth your time. Having an autonomous team in place to run your business is an essential step in firing yourself first. A great team is non-negotiable. It must be in place. The great news is the 11-step hiring process will help you locate the winners you're seeking for your team and avoid the duds. Once you have compiled your excellent team, you are well on your way to selling the business or creating your ATM.

Training Your Autonomous Team

You must train your team to operate without you. This can be tricky, but remember the goal is they need to be able to carry on smoothly without you! As the business owner, once you decide on your exit, you'll notice a shift in your role in the company. Your new role focuses on strategy and culture. You're no longer the operations guy—you have stepped away from making decisions. This shift could be difficult because you've trained your teams to wait for you before making decisions. if you've trained your staff to depend on you, they will. They might not want to make any decisions without you. Now you need to train them to not depend so heavily on you. That was my reality for many, many years. However, once I pushed through this limitation and trained my staff to operate without me, my business notably scaled. Not surprisingly, I suddenly had the free time to do what I wanted, not just what I had to.

Here are two tips to teach your company to operate without you:

Reassure them you will work two or three days a week in the business. However, their access to you will be very limited, so they'll have to solve problems on their own.

Encourage your team to take steps, make changes, and make their own decisions. If they throw a question your way, suggest they Google it first. With all of the available information, there is simply no reason why your team members can't do their research if they have a question. Teach them to rely on themselves, not on you, to solve problems or make decisions.

STEP 3

Dashboards and Scorecards

*You'll never know if you're winning
if you never keep score.*

N ow that you've taken the time to complete the first two
steps in the Fire Yourself First Process, by unearthing
your personal why and hiring your autonomous team,
now is the time to move on to step 3—ensuring that both
you and your team all know what winning looks like. The
tools I use to keep everyone on track are dashboards and
scorecards. Dashboards are for you, the owner, and your
senior leadership team, and scorecards are for your senior
leadership team's direct reports. Let's begin to unpack both
of these terms.

What Are Dashboards?

Driving down the road, it's easy to feel carefree as you gaze out into the horizon or glimpse the autumn leaves slowly fading from green to deep reds. But all of a sudden, that inner peace turns into panic if we spot a police officer out of the corner of our eye and think our joy ride might be taking a different path than the one we had expected. Thankfully, a glance at our dashboard eases our nerves. We check the speedometer and discover we weren't driving too fast and that inauspicious cop car disappears in the distance, along with our initial trepidation. In the same vein, having a dashboard for our businesses will give us a snapshot of the company's overall performance, bringing us a sense of peace that our business is operating well because the numbers show we aren't in danger.

Dashboards are for you, the business owner, and for your senior leadership team. Dashboards are also the easiest way to track the key metrics of your company. In step 2, you evaluated your team. During this third step, as you create your dashboards, you must evaluate your business's key numbers. At this point in the life of your company, you probably have key numbers your CFO or finance team sends you. However, now it's time to do a deeper dive and track the most important numbers in your business. These numbers will go on your dashboard and are the ones you track on a weekly or monthly basis to ensure your company is performing the way you desire.

Identifying the most important numbers in your business is essential, especially if you won't be present during the day-to-day operations. Another reason to review your current metrics, KPIs (key performance indictors), or OKRs (objectives and key results) is you will increase the valuation of your business if you choose to sell it. Even more, identifying these key numbers will give you peace of mind because you will always know whether your company is performing as it should. There's another reason for identifying your key numbers. They will act as a beacon for your team to follow and enable them to understand what winning looks like in your organization.

Begin first by developing a dashboard for yourself. As the owner, you need to track only three to five numbers, and your numbers will be different from everybody else's numbers. For instance, take your president. While his dashboard potentially includes your three to five numbers, he will have numbers for the people who directly report to him.

Everyone's dashboards are unique to each person's role in the company.

Once you have identified which three to five numbers belong on your personal dashboard, have your senior leadership team or managers create dashboards for their departments that feed into your dashboard. Your senior leadership team may have three key numbers on their dashboard that feed into one of yours. Perhaps one of your key numbers is gross profit. Your shipping department could have three key numbers on their dashboard that affect gross profit: one for deliveries, another for in-stock items, and the last for turnaround time. All three of those actions from the shipping department certainly affect the gross margin, but you, as the owner, don't need to have those numbers on your dashboard. While you certainly want those numbers tracked, that is something for the leadership in shipping to keep their eyes on. By keeping those numbers off your dashboard, it frees you up to track the most crucial three to five numbers in the business.

Regardless of which type of exit you take, what you don't want to happen is to go from working 40 to 60 hours a week to only 4 to 10 hours a month, and suddenly your revenue and gross profit dip. Even worse, what if your business expenses simultaneously increased? If all this starts to happen, then, Houston, we have a problem! If any of these scenarios occur, you'll find yourself dragged back into the business you were supposedly exiting. It's crucial to determine these key numbers now. Once you have created your dashboards, you will sleep at night knowing your business is doing well without you at the helm.

What Are Scorecards?

Imagine a basketball game where both teams are stocked with great players. The players run up and down the court, making great passes and quick shots. The game is exciting, and the action is quick. Then the scoreboard breaks. What would happen? After about two minutes of play, I wouldn't have a clue what the score was. The plays move too quickly to accurately keep track of the score. Who would win and who would lose if you couldn't keep score? The experience would be a letdown for players on both sides of the court. Similarly, most employees feel that way every day when they come to work—am I winning at my job or am I losing? Unfortunately, many employees don't understand what winning looks like because they don't know what's expected of them.

According to a *Harvard Business Review* study, 95 percent of employees don't understand what winning in their job looks like.[16] This reality makes successful execution at your organization nearly impossible. That number—95 percent of employees—is staggering and unacceptable if you plan to Fire Yourself First. It is up to you, as the owner, to ensure every team member understands your company's strategy and knows how to win in their roles.

You must strategically communicate your expectations to your team members and give give them key metrics to aim for. With these metrics in place, your employees can take ownership of their roles in your company. As stated in the *Harvard Business Review,*

> "The message should be two-fold: this is what we are trying to achieve and this is how we will measure if we are achieving it."[17]

How do we help our team members play to win? How do we help them understand your expectations? Simply by implementing scorecards.

While dashboards are for you and your senior leadership team, scorecards are for team members. Depending on their jobs, each team member will have specific, measurable numbers on their scorecard, so they know what winning looks like. For example, if you have an inventory control supervisor, this individual might have a scorecard that includes tracking re-order levels, backup suppliers, and accuracy in the computer systems. This team member's scorecard would identify what he needs to do to win in his position.

Dashboards and scorecards provide clarity to every person on the team because they all know what is expected of them. They will also know if they are doing a good job or not. Scorecards also allow supervisors and leaders the opportunity to touch base with team members who may be falling behind. Without a scorecard, a manager might not even know a team member needed assistance, but with a scorecard in place, it's apparent who's on track and who isn't.

Another benefit of the scorecard is if a team member is doing extremely well and crushing their goals, it provides an opportunity for leadership to congratulate and celebrate that person. In short, scorecards allow your employees to come to work fully engaged and feeling appreciated and happy—this is the natural result of knowing what's expected of them. Think about the kind of work environment you're creating. It's a place where your employees come in every single week, they feel appreciated, they are offered help, and they know what's expected of them. Setting up that kind of workplace culture is so valuable and how you keep long-term employees.

One of the worst things that could happen if you scaled back your time is to discover you were the business's GPS. While you didn't realize it at the time, every day, every person in your company checked in with you to see what was happening, whether they were doing a good job, or maybe even to learn what job they should be doing. This level of detail is not your responsibility as the owner, especially if you want to exit your company. Every person needs their own scorecard, so they know what they are responsible for at work. Scorecards give team members the ability to know beyond a shadow of a doubt how to win at work.

Scorecards give team members the ability to know beyond a shadow of a doubt how to win at work.

Once I implemented scorecards for my team members, I saw our revenues jump 30 percent! That proved to me they worked. One little change can have such a profound effect on your organization. As an added bonus, these positive results came quickly because the team learned what was expected of them every week and could respond to those expectations. This was truly a win-win situation!

Practical Tips for Implementation

Here's how to apply dashboards and scorecards in your business. In my medical clinic business, the clinic manager posts the weekly numbers every Monday morning on a group communication software we use called Slack. Note that my manager is posting the numbers—not me! Once the key numbers are posted, all other team members (and I) know whether they reached their goals for the previous week. In essence, everyone knows the score. We do this every week, so we have clarity on how we're doing. Even when I do come into the office, I stay only an hour or two during any given month, and it's usually to have lunch with a particular person or possibly a team lunch. I'm not there to ensure everyone is meeting goals. That's what the dashboards and scorecards are for. My team and I have something that quickly communicates how the business is doing and how individuals are performing. Without a doubt, dashboards and scorecards are efficient tools for a quick check-up on the business.

At this point in my life, I have fired myself first from all my businesses and work only a few days each month. At the same time, I earn more than I ever have before and enjoy more free time. Much of my work is going online and checking out the dashboards and scoreboards of my companies.

That's it.

While I do come in for an hour or two for a team lunch, to converse with my teams, and to see what's happening, for the most part, I'm working in my businesses by looking at the key numbers. That's my job now and where you can be too.

Picking Your Key Numbers

While dashboards and scorecards sound like great tools, there's always that difficult task of deciding *which* numbers to track. What *are* the most important numbers? What are the most critical *three to five numbers* I need to track on my dashboard?

To begin, choose numbers you think will allow you to see the true operational success of your business. Sometimes, it takes a few iterations to come up with the critical numbers, so don't be discouraged if you don't immediately know what to track. It may take you three, six, or even nine months to discover the "real" numbers. This is all part of the process of firing yourself first.

As you are transitioning in your role, give yourself time to figure out which numbers are your key numbers. That's why it's important to start now. It will give you time to adjust because, often, a number you thought was critical might turn out not to be so significant.

When creating a dashboard for yourself, you want it to be as simple as possible. You don't want to track fifteen key numbers—that's too many. Instead, track between three to five numbers. While this doesn't sound like a lot, when you take time to think deeply about your business and how it operates, you'll learn you can distill those fifteen numbers down to five. Think about the numbers that trigger other numbers. You're aiming for that first domino, the one that will knock down all the rest. In other words, pick a number impacted by other numbers.

For example, in one of my businesses, we found our Google online review rating directly impacts our revenue. The online review rating is a number I added to my dashboard and on every team member's scorecard. Why? I know for every .1 off of five on that Google rating, it will cost us tens of thousands of dollars every month. I could lose half my monthly revenue if we had a 4.1 ranking. That's how important that number is.

Over time, I've also learned most businesses want to target a 4.6 to 4.8 rating. Nobody believes in a five out of five rating, but they certainly believe in a 4.8 or 4.7. So, that is what I aim for. In addition to affecting revenue, many other numbers feed into the number of 5-star ratings we receive, including customer satisfaction and employee engagement. So, by tracking one number—the number of 5-star reviews we get—I gain a sense of what is going on in the business while I am not there.

While everybody's business will differ vastly from another, some key numbers should be on everyone's dashboard, regardless of the company. One would be gross profit (or profit margin if that is more important to your business). And while the percentage of profit is ultimately the number I care about, don't forget to take into consideration other numbers that drive your profit. You need to know those numbers because they can give you an early warning if you have a problem. This is partly why every Monday morning the leadership shares key numbers with the team. While a weekly posting may be a bit too often for you and your business, if I see a problem popped up from one week to the next, then I know we can follow up with team members and address the issue.

Here are some examples of other numbers you might track on your dashboard:

- Productivity
- Leakage
- Billing hours
- On-time shipping

What is unique to *your* business? That answer might provide some insight into the key numbers you need to track. Imagine you logged in from home or received an email summary from someone in the company, what numbers would they need to send you? What must you know about?

Once you've identified your dashboard numbers, soon you will only need to spend an hour or two every month looking at these high-level numbers. You'll immediately know the pulse of your business. That's the power of dashboards and scorecards—they communicate to you (and everyone else) what winning looks like. The clarity that comes from knowing how well your business is operating even without you at the helm will help you sleep better at night. It will also bring you another step closer to having a business where you get to choose how many hours you want to work. As a bonus, you will be able to sell your company at a higher valuation because you have systems in place that allow your business to run without you.

Designing Your Dashboard

Here is a series of questions to help people create their dashboards, regardless of the type of industry. You can download this how-to guide at www.FireYourselfFirst.com/resources.

The first step in this process is to reflect on *why* you should track your goals. Ask yourself:

- Why is having a business goal important?
- Why does it matter to you?
- To your team members?

What Should You Track?

To help you figure out what to track, ask yourself the following questions:

1. What is your goal for the company?
2. Why is that goal important?
3. What do you need to *do* to reach that goal?

Once you've answered those three questions, begin to create a dashboard with three or four measurable activities to help you reach your business's goal.

Where Are You Going?

Now, take some time to think about where your company is going and ask yourself the following questions:

1. Think three years out from now. Establish a goal for that future date (e.g., I'd like to see $2 million in new revenues, I'd like to be semi-retired).
2. Plan your goals/targets for this current year (e.g., $1.1 million in new revenues, 100 new customers).
3. What do you need to do in the next ninety days (e.g., hire three key people, create a webinar)?
4. What do you need to do in the next thirty days (e.g., notify current customers of a new product offering, implement sales training)?

Why Should You Track It?

Take some time to answer: Why is that goal important to:

1. You?
2. Your team?
3. Your customers?

Start Building the Plan

There are four rules to follow when building your plan:

1. Your plan must be clear and concise. You must be able to quickly put into words what your plan is. Think short and sweet.
2. Your plan must be measurable. For example, I need to hire two key managers, as opposed to I need to hire some team members.
3. Your plan needs to have an end date. I will accomplish X by Y date.
4. You need to articulate *who* will accomplish each part of the plan.

To sum it up, when you start building your plan, you establish, "I'm going to do **what**, by **when**."

Write Down the Plan

In this next section, take the time to write out your plan. Notice that you begin with your three-year goals and end with your thirty-day goals. Don't forget to apply my four rules when you write down your plan.

	Specific Goals	Who (is going to do it)?
3-year Goals	1. 2. 3.	
1-year Goals	1. 2. 3.	
90-day Goals	1. 2. 3.	
30-day Goals	1. 2. 3.	

Create the Dashboard to Track Success

There's a famous quote often attributed to W. Edwards Deming that says, "What gets measured, gets done." Your dashboard measures whether your company is reaching your goals. These goals can be financial, customer-related, or based on any other indicators you want to track. One final tip for creating dashboards—do not overcomplicate them. Instead, try to repurpose existing data you already have from your CRM, CPA, or data already created in Excel®, Google Sheets™, Word®, or Google Pages™.

Below is a sample dashboard that has four, clearly articulated goals. It articulates what I am aiming for (my goal), how the company is currently performing at the goal, and then tracks the variance between what I desire and where we are performing.

Goals	Goal	Current	Variance
Upgrade 50 customers to the new "Second Level" package	50/m	20	-30
Reduce Expenses by 25%	25%	30%	+5%
# of 5-Star reviews per month	225	225	0
Past customer email mail campaign (# emails sent)	1,500	0	-1,500

After seeing a sample dashboard and completing your goal planning, try to create your dashboard using the following template.

Goals	Goal	Current	Variance

Create Team Goals with a Scorecard

Let's begin working on scorecards for your other team members. Be sure to post your scorecards for everyone to see. Each team member needs to know whether they are winning. Feel free to use any program you'd like to keep track of your scorecards (e.g., Word, Excel).

Below is a sample scorecard for a team member. Be clear and specific about what you expect from your team members and communicate it to them through their scorecards.

The goals ask for a specific number from team members per goal. Help your team members know how to win at work by telling exactly how many customers they need to email. Be specific about the number of customer packages they need to sell. You are not doing them any favors by being vague. On the flip side, by giving clear, specific goals, you help them win and feel confident at work.

Monthly Goals	Goal Per Week	Actual
Sell 8 customers to the new "Second Level" package	2	
Upsell 4 "Starter Package" customers with a service agreement	1	
# of 5-Star reviews per month	5	
Past customer email mail campaign (# emails sent)	375 emails	

After seeing a sample scorecard, take some time to create a scorecard for one of your team members using the following template.

Goals	Goal Per Week	Actual

The Goal of Goals

As the American author, salesman, and motivational speaker Zig Ziglar once said, "If you aim at nothing, you'll hit it every time."[18] For any business owner, it is imperative to have goals for your company. They give you and your team members something to aim for. Everyone on your team wants to know why your business is doing what it's doing. They also want to know what they should be doing in their roles. As the owner, you should look ahead and determine where your business is heading thirty days from now up to three years in the future. Write down your goals and measurements for the company and share them with your team members. By doing so, you bring clarity to an oftentimes unclear environment.

When you create dashboards and scorecards, you're setting up your business and team members for success. It also happens to be another step that will enable you to fire yourself first.

STEP 4

Your Autonomous Exit

Creating a business that runs without you gives you the freedom to choose a life you love.

t last, you have reached the final step in the Fire Yourself First Process—your autonomous exit. This final step is personal and will result in different paths depending on your goals. I've dubbed this last step your "autonomous exit" for two reasons. First, autonomous refers to the kind of business you will set up regardless of the exit you take. Your business will run smoothly and generate an income for you, without you there in the day-in and day-out operations. What has enabled your business to reach this point is you will have hired and trained the right teams and implemented your dashboards and scorecards. With those in place, you are free to begin your autonomous exit.

Second, your autonomous exit refers to your personal autonomy coming as a result of creating your self-running company. By creating an autonomous company that generates revenue for you, you have given yourself the gift of autonomy—the capacity to decide for yourself what you'd like to do with your company and what kind of exit you're interested in pursuing.

Everyone will exit his or her company at some point. So, wouldn't it be nice to have a choice in the matter? Wouldn't it be great to set up your company in such a way that *you* decide when to sell or scale back your time in the business? As the person who had the idea for the company in the first place, who built the business, and who worked all of those long hours, don't you deserve a choice? Don't you want to be able to choose when to sell your company, as opposed to being forced to sell because of illness or another catastrophic event that takes you out of the game? That's why you need to fire yourself first because you offer yourself the gift of freedom.

Are You Ready to Exit?

It's always helpful to know the signs of readiness, and you may already see signs you are ready to exit your company. However, being ready to exit won't happen overnight. It often takes roughly one to three years to get your business to the point in the Fire Yourself First Process where you can begin to exit. How long will it take? How long the process takes is up to you. For instance, do you feel an urgent call to exit your business? In this case, you'll probably work through the first three steps of my Fire Yourself First Process more quickly than someone who is just beginning to consider their future exit. Either way, do not feel pressure to get through the process in a certain number of years. It's better to have time to plan and be able to adjust your plan than to hurry the process. As we all know, anytime you rush a project, things don't end up happening the way they are supposed to and something frequently goes amiss.

What needs to be in place to ensure a successful exit?

1. You need to demonstrate a solid historical performance from your company. Your company needs to be operating well, and it needs to have done so for a while.
2. Once you've considered your track record, ensure your business has opportunities for future growth. Your business must be able to move forward and grow alongside our ever-changing world. Remaining stagnant is not an option.
3. You need plans for the company's future growth, along with a management team and excellent systems in place.
4. You need to complete both a business and a customer risk assessment.
5. Your business should be autonomous—running without you at the helm.

You also need to think about what *you* need to have in place before you exit. In essence, you need to get your financial house in order because, regardless of the exit you choose, you must make sure you're financially set.

Here's what you need to personally have in place:

1. Have a financial plan. How much money do you need to live each year? Is there a certain amount of money you're hoping to receive upon your exit? What is your exit amount?

2. Have a plan for your family, which may include a trust. What about your estate plans? Do you know how that will be passed on? Have you met with an estate planner?
3. Consider your charitable giving and insurance planning. Do you have the insurance coverage you need?

There is much in your own financial life to consider and get in line before you can exit your business. By doing so, you'll set yourself and your loved ones up for a successful exit.

Selecting Your Exit

While the world went through the Covid-19 pandemic, many changes happened in the workplace. We witnessed employees who would commute daily to the office suddenly stay at home to work. And while many businesses eventually returned to the office model or implemented a hybrid model, undoubtedly, the pandemic profoundly impacted the workplace. The Covid pandemic proved I didn't have to physically be at work eighty hours a week for my business to succeed. So, in some strange turn of events, the pandemic helped me to reimagine what running a business looks like.

As I mentioned at the very beginning of the book, there are three general exits: six feet under, setting up an ATM so the business runs without you, and selling your business at the highest valuation. Nobody desires the first exit, so let's plan for option two or three.

Both of those choices—the ATM or the sale—are personal decisions. Make this decision after carefully considering what is best for you and your family. Unfortunately, we are often not in sync with our families and with what they want, so start discussions with your family early. Begin by asking them questions. How do they see the next two to five years? Where would they like to be ten years from now? By having these discussions with your family, you will gain a better grasp on which type of exit you should take. You also have the benefit of addressing the concerns and feelings of those closest to you.

Part of the difficulty with exits is there are several ways to do so. There is not one "correct" exit strategy. This is not a one size fits all situation. Instead, there is an exit spectrum with completely selling your business on one end and working a couple of hours a month at the other. What lies between is a variety of choices.

Where do you want to fall on that exit spectrum? What would suit you best? While it's true that at some point in your life you will sell your business, that sale doesn't have to happen right now. You could wait until you're in your nineties to sell. Another option would be to sell your company now to start a new business venture. Honestly, you have many options to choose from.

For many business owners, there is only one way to exit—sell the business. But, just as the pandemic opened my eyes to a new way of running a business, you have more than one way to exit. For example, do you want to sell to try a new business? Do you desire a "mini exit" where you scale back tremendously while maintaining ownership? What are you interested in doing?

Think outside the box. Sometimes when you begin to think in a new way, a realm of possibilities you never even dreamt of comes to life. For example, one attendee at my live events was interested in opening an aesthetic practice. That was his goal and why he came. However, when he heard me encouraging everyone there to think outside of the box, he went in a completely different direction. Instead of finding a new location for his clinic, he decided to buy a tattoo parlor whose owner was retiring. He planned to add aesthetics to the services already offered to those more than 10,000 customers. This individual loved doing laser tattoo removal, and this procedure easily went hand in hand with the business's existing tattoo services. The last I heard, this individual had opened up four locations, and he did so all because he finally began to think outside of the box.

Don't limit yourself by thinking your exit can go in only one direction.

Think creatively.

Reimagine what an exit could be.

Consider all the possibilities.

This fourth step in the Fire Yourself First Process is simply about taking the time to think about what you want. However, sometimes all the options overwhelm us, so think about it this way. To some extent, you have only two options, which happen to be either end of the exit spectrum: the sale or the ATM. So, what do you desire to do with your company? Your business is a large portion of your legacy. It's what you built. It's where you logged all those long hours. It's what will provide you with your new adventure, because, regardless of which exit you choose, you'll have additional resources and time at your disposal. In the end, your autonomous exit is about you, your life, and your dreams. Do what works for you.

Examining the ATM

Let's consider a potential ATM exit where your business is running without you. If you set up your company as an ATM, you have the benefit of not having to work much, you're still generating income, and you get your freedom back. It has the added benefit that when you finally do sell, you'll receive a better valuation on your business.

Why else would people choose to set up their business as an ATM? This option is for those who aren't quite ready to give up their businesses. I've chosen this option because I love my businesses. I'm not tired of them, and I'm still passionate about my work. I'm not ready to give them up and want to be a part of them, to a small degree. Teams run my businesses, which allows me to participate when I want. Sometimes I may work more. Sometimes I work less.

But the great news is I have the choice.

Whether I'm excited about a new project and want to be more involved, I can. If I desire to take a week or two to travel or do something less exotic, such as reading books and biking around my neighborhood, I have the option.

What is the one key that drives the ATM exit? You cannot be the center of your business anymore. You cannot be the linchpin. You must fire yourself first. When you do, you get to sit back and watch your business run without you. Then, you can tweak your company here or there if you need to. If you realize you've made a mistake, go back to the drawing board and fix it because you have the time.

If you desire this kind of exit, set a goal for yourself. For example, your goal could be to work only two to five hours a month. Once you grasp the amount of time you want to spend in the business, you must also consider what your involvement in your company will look like.

Ask yourself:

- If you work two hours a month, how often will you go to the office?

- Will you go in at all?
- If you do, for what purpose are you going?
- Will you work from home?
- On what?

These are all things to consider if you scale back your time and set up your ATM.

Examining the Sale

If you choose this route, once you have sold your business, that's the end. Your exit is complete. You are out of the business, which is what you were seeking.

You have many options when it comes to selling your business.

1. You could liquidate the business to generate cash.
2. You have the option to sell it privately to a person, a private equity firm, or a venture capital group.
3. You could sell it to family members, to your employees, or to your managers.
4. You could go public and become a publicly traded and owned company.

A quick thought about selling to family members: if you choose to go this route, you must ensure your company is running smoothly as an ATM. In other words, your company must not rely on you (or a potential family member) to run the business. Why? Oftentimes, the second generation that runs a company doesn't do as good of a job. This isn't always the case, but I've seen it happen time and time again when a father created a business and ran it successfully, only to have his son acquire it and run it into the ground. So, be careful when selling to your family. It's not that you can't do so, but remember, you are trying to get the best valuation for your business and the best return for all your hard work.

Most likely if you sell your business, you'll receive a big shock once you've exited your company completely. Suddenly, you will have opened up a world of excess time and money, but you may be surprised to discover you feel a bit uneasy—you're uncertain about where to go and what to do. You might even find yourself struggling with uncertainty and unhappiness, while your spouse is happy with the change. And that might feel unfair—after all, you're the one who built the business. You're the one who logged all those long hours. When do *you* get the chance to be happy?

Should you find yourself in this situation, you need to participate in the upside. Ask yourself, what is the upside of selling my business?

While you have "lost" your position in your company, "lost" your daily schedule, and "lost" a variety of other things that came with running your company, now is the time to think about the upside—what have you gained in the sale of your company? What do you have now that you've never had before? What were the perks of selling?

Don't focus on your losses. Focus on what you have gained.

Earning the Highest Valuation: The Strategic Exit

If you plan to sell, your business valuation will be very important. Just as the 11-step hiring process is extremely thorough to ensure you're hiring the all-stars and avoiding the duds, you need to be incredibly thorough and involved in your exit. You have access to an enormous amount of information about the exit process, from podcasts to books to mentors and so on, and you must allocate time to learn about it. Don't hand over your exit to a consultant and let them do all the work. While you can have a consultant execute many of the boring details involved in selling your company, you still need to take ownership of the sale. It is your company. It is your sale. And don't believe everything you hear from your consultant. Do your research and learn the ins and outs of selling your business or it could cost you.

> **Do your research and learn the ins and outs of selling your business or it could cost you.**

You are looking for a strategic buyer, and truth be told, usually we do need some help finding the best buyer for our business. That is why the specifics of a business valuation should be left to a third party—someone who will help us think outside of the box. Usually, the owner is too involved to get the best valuation. We need someone else to help us in the process because you may think of two or three people who could be your buyers. However, a third-party expert could find someone completely different to buy your business.

These experts show you what is possible by considering everything and trying to maximize your valuation. When you sell your business, look for that strategic buyer who thinks, "One plus one equals eleven!" This could occur because your potential buyer realizes he could double his current revenue simply by adding your business or by modifying what you're already offering. Oftentimes, this kind of strategic buyer isn't aware of your business until you put it up for sale. This person probably isn't on your radar.

You most likely will have a list of people who may want to buy your business. Perhaps some have expressed an interest in buying. However, that does not mean they are the best people to buy your company. We are looking for a strategic exit with a strategic buyer—the buyer who will give us the highest valuation.

Many years ago, I met an entrepreneur who owned a chain of yogurt stores in southern California. Most people imagine the typical buyer for a yogurt store would be another yogurt chain, right? This way, the buyer would double their business, and the owner would likely get a good price for their company. But this situation isn't ideal. It's more like a one plus one equals (maybe) three. Perhaps in this particular industry, that valuation would be typical, which means the owner would get a two- or three-times valuation, but nothing more.

In the case of this yogurt entrepreneur, he ended up selling to an "unusual" buyer—a farm. By doing so, he received an incredible ten times multiple for his business rather than a two times multiple. He was able to think outside of the box. You see, the farm could produce the raw material needed for the yogurt: milk. By using their milk, the farm's raw costs were much lower than those of my entrepreneur friend. Perhaps he was paying one dollar for a gallon of milk, but for the farm, its actual cost per gallon was a mere ten cents! The farm was willing to pay a higher valuation for the stores because the yogurt business enabled them to distribute their raw product at a higher selling price.

We need to think outside of the box when we are selling our businesses.

As the owner, we can be a little too close to our business and a little too confined in our work sphere to identify all of the opportunities in front of us. We might foolishly think the only buyer for our yogurt business would be another yogurt business. But we'd be wrong. That's why a good broker or expert in strategic acquisitions is in order when you go to sell your business. The fees they charge will pay for themselves many times over because the experience they bring to the table and the selling price they are able to obtain for your business will be worth it. In other words, don't be cheap. Don't be penny wise and pound foolish. Hire a professional to help you with your sale.

If your industry is one where owners tend to get a two-time valuation, tell your broker or acquisitions expert they can earn a percentage of anything over a two-time valuation. This kind of negotiation is necessary and will protect you against bad brokers and people who *think* they are experts.

When it comes to selling, you're walking through a minefield. Pay attention and be on the lookout for consultants looking to make a quick buck. Be careful, be strategic, and be aware. When you have fired yourself first and ensured your business can run without you, you're on track to the dream scenario of one plus one equals eleven. When this happens, a potential buyer can plug your company into their big system. In the real world, that's where the big valuations are.

Planning Your Exit

As Benjamin Franklin once said, "If you fail to plan, you are planning to fail."[19] When it comes to successfully exiting your business, you need to have a plan. You never know when your health is going to get away from you. You never know when something completely out of your control could happen. If it does, you may find yourself in a desperate situation. As the saying goes, desperate times call for desperate measures, and you may sell to the first buyer who comes along, regardless of the deal.

I once knew someone involved in a terrible accident that resulted in many neurological problems. It left him unable to work. This individual thought he had plenty of years to work and plan his exit. He suddenly found himself in a precarious situation. Instead of having the opportunity to find a strategic buyer and get the most for his company, he began liquidating his business and selling everything at cost. He experienced loss on multiple fronts: the health losses from the accident and the financial losses from having to sell his business quickly, rather than strategically.

Take the time to plan your strategic exit. Start thinking about who a potential buyer for your business could be. If you haven't done any research or any planning and tragedy strikes, you will be forced to sell to the first buyer who offers you money. We all exit. It's just when we do that's unknown. Think about what you personally need to do to exit. What does your business need to have in place for you to exit? Don't forget to set up your exit in such a way that you get the highest valuation.

Your business is a part of your legacy. Don't let all your hard work go to waste. Get the most out of your time and effort by carefully planning your exit. Start restructuring your business to run without you as soon as you can because, in the final analysis, that's the key to a successful exit.

PART THREE

Do What You Love Next

What Comes Next?

Once you've reached the point of freedom, whether you've sold your business or set it up as a personal ATM, it follows that you would ask yourself, "What comes next?" If you have the freedom to work two or three days a month, what do you want to do with the rest of the time? For some, the fear of the unknown could stop them from selling their company or running it as an ATM because they have no clue what they would do next.

What could you do with your newfound freedom?

Could you create a brand-new business?

Spend more time with your family?

Give more money to charity?

Travel to places you've always dreamt of visiting?

You could become a lifestyle investor like author Justin Donald, whose investments generate enough money for him to live his dream life.[20] The good news is once you have fired yourself first, you have the option to choose a new path. After all, the business is working for you, instead of you working for the business. You've given yourself the time to work *on* your business, instead of *in* your business.

From this point on, I don't have a simple system I can share or advice for you to follow. What I can do is recount my journey of exiting my businesses and what it's like experiencing the freedom, openness, and availability in my once-busy schedule. Hopefully, upon hearing the steps I've taken and the opportunities that have come my way, it will inspire you on this final part of your journey. We all desire to do what we love, and my goal in writing this book is to enable you to do just that—pursue your passions, pursue your dreams, and pursue your loves. I'm excited to show you what is possible.

Attaining Self-Actualization

Mahatma Gandhi. Steve Jobs. Mother Theresa. Even though their time has come and gone here on earth, we still know their names and still value their impact. Have you ever thought about why that is? Why are we so impressed by others who have left a lasting impact? Why do their names carry on throughout the ages, becoming known to new generations as older generations fade away? Ultimately, we are all wired to contribute to the world and to leave a lasting impact on those around us.

The idea that we all desire to contribute is not new. Abraham Maslow, a famous American psychologist, documented this universal human tendency in his famous hierarchy of needs. As Maslow noted, humans have a variety of needs. At the most basic level, we have physiological needs for things such as food, water, and shelter. Once we meet our first level of physiological needs, we move up to the next and more complex level of human needs—safety and security. As Maslow's theory claims, we continue to journey up this hierarchy of needs until we reach the pinnacle and the most complex human need: self-actualization. This final need—self-actualization—is where we become self-aware and concerned with our personal growth. We become less concerned with the opinions of others and more concerned with fulfilling our potential. We desire to be all we can be. As we all know, the desire for humans to progress in life is normal. No one desires to remain at the bottom of the pyramid for the entirety of their lives.

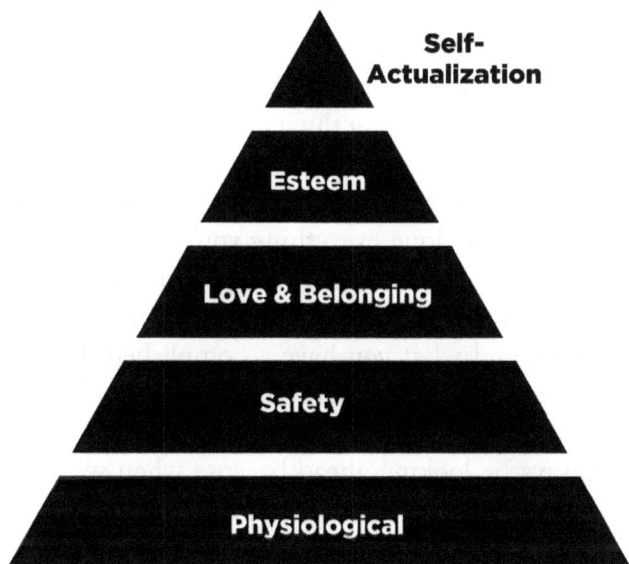

Self-
Actualization

Esteem

Love & Belonging

Safety

Physiological

When you finally reach the top of Maslow's hierarchy of needs, you no longer run in the rat race. At the point of self-actualization, you desire to become something better. For the entrepreneur, you will have accomplished your major life and business goals. You now look to see what is next.

Oftentimes, this curiosity about the future and a desire for personal growth begins with the feeling of being unsettled. This happens because you have "reached the top" and believe you should be happy because you have everything you are "supposed" to have. But you don't.

Something is missing.

But what is missing? I'm here to help you discover what comes next once you've finally reached the point of self-actualization. I'm hoping I can help you see you're just beginning a great, new adventure.

Focus on the Gain

When you have finally reached the top of the mountain, it's easy to look around, take in the incredible view, and begin to think about your descent—the slow trudge back down the mountain. But this point in your professional and personal life—when you've done everything you've sought to do—is actually when you could begin your greatest journey. You've reached the stage of self-actualization. You finally accept who you are and what you have accomplished. In *The Gap and the Gain*, authors Dan Sullivan and Dr. Benjamin Hardy discuss the reality that it can be quite disheartening for people to always be looking ahead because when we do so, we never feel as though we have accomplished anything. Instead, we're always looking for the "gap" in our lives.[21] They go on to say the key is to look back and examine what it is you have accomplished. This is our true "gain."

To help you focus on your many gains in life, you may find it helpful to journal about where you were ten years ago.

- Where did you live?
- What did you drive?

- How did your family look?
- How did your business or professional life look?
- What kept you up at night?

Now, jump forward to today.

- Where are you living?
- What are you driving?
- Do you have any other homes?
- How does your family look?
- How does your business look?
- How do you spend your time?

Most likely, when you compare these two different times, you will realize you have much to celebrate. There have been many gains in your life!

Let's return to that unsettled feeling from earlier, the one that came at the point of self-actualization. What lies underneath this emotion? It's your lack of control coming into play. When you were running your business, you knew precisely what you needed to do. You put into action the steps to get it done, which gave you a sense of control. But at this stage in the game, once you have fired yourself first, everything is different. And while you have accomplished your major goals in life, you remain unsatisfied.

If you are a high-performing individual, this feeling is completely normal, so breathe easy. This is how many people who have walked this path before you have felt. I became restless for the first six months to a year after I had fired myself first. Even though it was an exciting time in my life, that feeling of uncertainty accompanied my newfound freedom. Often people begin to placate this unsettled feeling by jumping back into their businesses. This strategy might work for a while. Eventually you will see it hinders you from getting to your next adventure. Remember, your work role has changed but you still have a purpose.

Your purpose is merely evolving, not disintegrating.

Life Beyond the Business

Once you have accepted there is life beyond the office, you can start your new journey. But before you can begin this new endeavor, you need the time to pursue it. If you are still running a business, your first critical step is to fire yourself first. When you do, you can reinvest the time spent at work into your new journey in life.

As you implement my 4-step Fire Yourself First Process, start thinking about what is next for you. Maybe you know what you want to do. If so, that is incredible! However, here's a fair warning: as you accomplish these initial goals, you will probably discover you want to do more. This is normal for the high achiever. Prepare yourself that you'll probably have to complete this process of discovering "what's next" several times.

Just as our autonomous exits look different depending on the individual, the "what's next" will also look different. Some will desire to play golf every week with their friends from high school. Go for it! Others will travel the world from east to west. Go for it! Maybe for you, family will be the center of your new journey and having monthly dates with your children and grandchildren will be your most important goal. Others want to live a life of experiences, so they will seek out adventures such as attending a culinary school in Italy or hiking Mount Kilimanjaro.

This is the time to plan all those bucket list activities or trips you have postponed because you lacked the time. Here's something to ponder:

- Once you check off the activities on your bucket list, do you think you will be happy?
- Will you feel satisfied?
- Will you have, what I like to call, Lived a Life Well Lived?

I'm not saying you shouldn't do those activities or take those trips. But sometimes, the activities and experiences are not what is missing in your life. There is something more you're seeking.

So, ask yourself:

- When you look back on your life from this moment in time, can you honestly say you lived a life well lived?
- Did you accomplish what you wanted?
- Did you even do what you wanted?
- Were you able to become the person you always dreamed of becoming?

If not, then *now* is the time to begin.

Helping others enables me to live a life well lived. As I mentioned earlier, my purpose statement is "to make a positive difference in people's lives by encouraging them to see what they cannot see by serving as their guide." I have accomplished this purpose in both my business and my personal life. So, for me, my "what's next" centers on fulfilling my purpose statement. It wasn't a bucket list that enabled me to live a life well lived.

It began with knowing my purpose.

People's Hunger for Purpose

Purpose is a topic that seems to randomly pop up in my conversations. People are hungry for purpose. The other day, one of my team members shared a story about her mother. Her mother lives on her own but has a few health problems. Her daughter frequently visits her to offer help. This mother is a retired woman in her seventies, and she is still looking for her purpose. Sadly, she just doesn't know what it is. This lack of knowledge causes her to feel depressed and insignificant.

I recommended the daughter ask her mom, "Whom would she like to help?"

This question is one you may want to ask yourself, too. When we think about how we can help others, we begin to understand our purpose. Another question we can ask is, "What superpower do I have?" Oftentimes, because we use our natural abilities so easily, we tend to be skeptical of them, undervalue them, and deem them insignificant. We imagine only something difficult would be of any real value. This isn't true.

Your natural abilities are unique, valuable, and unnatural for someone else. If you want to understand your purpose, start with your abilities.

What can you do well?

What comes easily to you?

In what areas do you excel?

Now, think about whom you could help with your superpowers.

Take this seventy-year-old retired mother. Perhaps she loves books, has always loved books, and just can't get enough of them. She could be a great reader and help out at the local library. Perhaps some children need someone to help them with their reading. Who better to help them than a woman who loves books, excels at reading, and could instill her love of reading in them? When you stop to consider who might benefit from your skills, you might discover your purpose.

Take some time to consider what you are passionate about. How could your passions be linked to your purpose? If you have already written a personal purpose statement, take it out and reread it. You are looking for something different—your what's next—and your mind will try and solve for that particular problem.

In the past, your personal purpose statement guided you. Now, reuse that same purpose statement to help you discover what comes next. If you don't have a personal statement of any kind and aren't sure where to begin, the following 4-step exercise may help.

1. Ask yourself: What do I already enjoy doing that I can do for hours and hours and the time just seems to fly by? Are there any specific topics I enjoy reading, listening to, or learning about? How could I help others with my unique skill set? How could I help others with one of my hobbies?

2. Recruit others for help by asking what they think you are good at doing. Oftentimes, what others think we do well is where we excel.

3. Find people whom you perceive as successful and ask what lights them up and excites them. Learning about someone else's passions might give insight into your own.

4. Find a quiet place, take a piece of blank paper, and at the top write "What's Next?" Pause for twenty seconds, take three huge, deep breaths, and start writing what comes to mind. (Don't edit yourself as you go,

or you'll disrupt your stream of consciousness. Just write!)

Once you have some ideas, try and edit them into one succinct sentence. Anything longer than that is too long. Then, rework your sentence into different variations until it begins to resonate with you. I find it helpful to set aside this sentence for a week. Then come back and look at it with fresh eyes.

Imagining What's Possible

The possibilities about what you could do, whom you could help, and how you could use your unique gifts seem endless. You'll be amazed at the ideas you can come up with and the opportunities you'll encounter once you have the time and freedom to pursue them. For example, I have reached the point where I've fired myself from all of my businesses. I currently work a total of ten days per month. One benefit of having down days in my schedule is I'm available for lunch meetings, and sometimes I'll find myself investing in an apartment complex as a result of one of those lunches. It's a wonderful, paradoxical scenario where I can earn more income while I work less. Also, I can multiply my impact on others and the world around me. You see, my journey didn't end when I fired myself first.

My journey began.

I'm blessed to do what I love in many different areas. For instance, I am passionate about helping those who cannot help themselves. They are often children. I've mentored high school students. I've helped build orphanages in India. I also train physicians to create profitable practices that will run without them, and I've become a whiskey expert along the way.

My father is an Army veteran, so I'm drawn to help veterans, especially by partnering with local veteran food banks. I like bringing the meals to others at the food bank. I like bringing dessert most of all because I love seeing the joy on people's faces when they get their end-of-meal sweets. I also have the opportunity to use my expertise to teach other businessmen how to run their operations more smoothly. These are a few of the ways I enjoy and find purpose in my freedom.

How do you choose what to pour your time and resources into? If I can help others with my unique skill set, which may include the money my skill set generates, I go for it. If it feels right in my "gut," I go for it. Combine your passions with your purpose. Start by asking yourself those hard questions, such as, "Am I living a well-lived life?"

Go further and ask yourself, "When I look back at my life, will I be able to say I did what I really wanted to do?"

Revisiting Your Purpose (Again and Again)

Your purpose, personal why, and discovery of what you want to do with your newfound freedom will inevitably change over time. It certainly did for me. One of my endeavors after I fired myself first was helping orphans in India. When I first went to India, I was overcome by many of the things I encountered. I had never been to a developing country before, and it was painful to witness some of the things I did. I saw a man dragging himself up and down the streets because he had no lower limbs and no healthcare system to turn to. I was astonished by the level of poverty. It was something I had never seen firsthand.

This experience in India impacted me so profoundly that I did further research and learned there are around 30 million orphans in India. This is an astronomical number. I set a goal to place some of those orphans in a safe shelter. This passion for helping those in need led me to connect with a philanthropic group called Angel House, which provides homes for orphans in India. Through Angel House, I used the resources I had earned from my companies to help build an orphanage in Malkajgiri, India. It is still in operation today. As the children grow up and become adults, the orphanage continues to help even more children.

It is a gift that keeps on giving.

Throughout this journey of building an orphanage, I fulfilled my personal why of helping others by giving these children a better life than the one they had. From time to time, I received videos from the orphanage showing children in their new home. These videos left me in tears. It was so wonderful to be a part of this work of helping the less fortunate. I was able to use my skills and abilities to help others who were in desperate need.

But over time, something changed and the work I was doing didn't have the same effect on me. I started feeling a little unsettled all over again. What I realized in this journey of helping others and finding purpose is I evolved—and this included how I gave and served others with my newfound freedom. When those unsettled feelings came, I recognized I had to take the time and revisit what I was doing and why.

When I did so, I discovered I wanted to be more present for my family and friends. My focus changed. Although I was still interested in helping and contributing to others, I felt an overwhelming urge to spend more time with my family and friends. I felt compelled to put them first in my life.

This change is all part of the ebb and flow of life. Recognize that things will change over time. This includes how you fulfill your purpose.

How do you tell whether a needed change is on the horizon? How do you detect if you need to reconsider your "What's Next?" An early warning that something needs to change is feeling unsettled. When that unsettled feeling comes and you can't shake it, you need to revisit what you are doing. Even if you are doing wonderful things, there may come a time when you feel urged to move onto something else. While you shouldn't change your purpose every three to six months, over time, you will probably revisit your purpose.

It's all part of the process.

Anticipate these unsettled feelings that may come your way. If they do rear their head, they are a normal part of the journey. Once you've fired yourself first, you don't need to know precisely what you are going to do for the rest of your days on earth. The truth is, you don't and can't know every single thing you're going to do because your purpose will change over the years. Take time to be inspired by the stories of others. Take time to think of the possibilities.

Give yourself the chance to dream again.

You don't have to figure it all out right away. You're on a journey. It is a journey that rewards you.

Moving Forward

Now is the time to try out a variety of avenues as you pursue your purpose and see how these different endeavors feel. Some things you choose will immediately feel right, and others will not seem authentic. The pursuit of "What's next?" will not happen overnight. In the real world, you will try some things.

Some of them will work.

Others will not.

There is no right or wrong way to do it. Give yourself permission to start a new journey and let it evolve (along with you) as you go down this new path. It's okay to make mistakes and to backtrack. It's even okay to start over. This is your life, which means you can live it the way you want to. You deserve to live a life well lived.

Even after you have carved out a path for yourself that you love, you're likely to reexamine your purpose from time to time. That's natural, and I'd love the opportunity to continue to serve as your guide along the way. If you would like some additional help throughout this process, please sign up for my weekly "Fire Yourself Friday," which is a short, five-minute-read email to keep you focused and moving forward.

I'm excited to see what path you forge in the future, and it all begins when you learn to fire yourself first.

To sign up for the free weekly email, visit
www.FireYourselfFirst.com/Friday

Afterword

I am committed to the idea that life is an experience, and experience matters. I'm so passionate about my life experience and living a purposeful life that even when I choose the mug I'm going to use on any given day, I think about how I'm feeling (or desire to feel) and choose my mug accordingly. For instance, I own a Yeti tumbler in the color Offshore Blue, and it's a gorgeous, deep blue with a hint of violet (in fact, it's the blue used on the front cover of this book). This particular shade of blue happens to be my mug of choice when I desire to get into the creative mindset. I'm not sure why this particular shade of blue strikes me in such a way, but it's my go-to choice whenever I want to create. On the other hand, I have a muted red mug I use when I desire to sit outside, possibly around a fire, and relax. Even that simple detail—what mug should I use—is an experience in the making. While others might just grab a mug and move on, that brief cup selection is more than just a drink for me. It's about choosing what kind of experience I desire because I know that - experience matters. In the end, I hope that when you pick up this book, both its contents and cover are a friendly reminder to think about the experience life has to offer you. If you're not currently enjoying your life's experience, then know you have it within you to choose a different path, to see something that, perhaps, you never noticed before, and to begin living a life well lived.

A Final Note to the Reader (and some Words of Hope)

As a business owner, the journey can be very lonely and unrewarding at times. It's natural to feel some discomfort, but it's also essential to know when that feeling is abnormal.

According to *Forbes*, the biggest predictor of suicide may not be depression or thoughts about killing yourself (what people in mental health call "suicidal ideation") but the feeling of being trapped.[22]

If you are struggling and feeling overwhelmed, it's important to reach out to your friends, family, or colleagues. The fact is, what you are feeling has been felt by others in the past, and you will feel it again in the future. Having a process to recognize and get help when you need it is critical. You may want to keep this from your family, but please tell your spouse or partner. It's important to have your #1 ally in your corner, and I guarantee you they will be grateful for you sharing this with them. Having help is an important part of managing this stress.

Fortunately, when you think about your network, you have more options than you may think. There are many peer groups like Vistage, EO, YPO, EntreLeadership, and your Chamber of Commerce. These groups often have a leader or facilitator, and please reach out to them. I promise you that you are not the first person to feel absolutely overwhelmed by the world. Also, you can reach out to your church, Rotary Club, or another group of which you are a member. If you have health benefits, you may also have additional confidential resources you can access.

As well, the 988 Suicide & Crisis Lifeline is a national network of local crisis centers that provides free and confidential emotional support to people in suicidal crisis or emotional distress 24 hours a day, seven days a week in the United States. Just dial 988 from any phone to access this service. If you are in Canada, call Talk Suicide Canada at 1-833-456-4566 (they have a 3-digit number coming soon).

Notes

1. "69 Troubling Workplace Statistics for 2022," Shortlisted, accessed September 2022, https://www.myshortlister.com/insights/workplace-stress-statistics.

2. "What is an Autonomous Car?" Synopsis, accessed October 2022, https://www.synopsys.com/automotive/what-is-autonomous-car.html.

3. Stephen R. Covey. *The Seven Habits of Highly Effective People*. New York: Free Press. 1989.

4. "Why 90% of Businesses Never Sell." *Tampa Business Broker* (blog). 2023. https://www.tampabusinessbroker.com/why-90-of-businesses-never-sell/.

5. Amy Gallo, "Making Your Strategy Work on the Frontline," Harvard Business Review, last modified June 24, 2010, https://hbr.org/2010/06/making-your-strategy-work-on-t.

6. Bo Burlingham, *Finish Big: How Great Entrepreneurs Exit Their Companies on Top* (New York, NY: Portfolio, 2014).

7. "The 9 Whys." WHY Institute. 2023. https://whyinstitute.com/right-way/

8. Dan Sullivan and Dr. Benjamin Hardy, *Who Not How: The Formula to Achieve Bigger Goals Through Accelerating Teamwork* (Carlsbad, CA: Hay House Business, 2020).

9. Cameron Herold, *Vivid Vision* (Carson City, NV: Lioncrest Publishing, 2020).

10. Cameron Herold, *Vivid Vision* (Carson City, NV: Lioncrest Publishing, 2020).

11. Patrick Lencioni, *The Ideal Team Player: How to Recognize and Cultivate The Three Essential Virtues* (San Francisco, CA: Jossey-Bass, 2016).

12. Rebekah Cardenas, "What's the Real Cost of a Bad Hire?" HR Exchange Network, last modified April 2, 2014, https://www.hrexchangenetwork.com/hr-talent-acquisition/articles/what-s-the-real-cost-of-a-bad-hire.

13. Shannon Waller, "Your Team Success," accessed November 2022, https://yourteamsuccess.com/.

14. CliftonStrengths, www.gallupstrengthscenter.com.

15. Kolbe Corp, https://www.kolbe.com/our-approach/.

16. Amy Gallo, "Making Your Strategy Work on the Frontline," accessed November 2022, https://hbr.org/2010/06/making-your-strategy-work-on-t.

17. Amy Gallo, "Making Your Strategy Work on the Frontline," accessed November 2022, https://hbr.org/2010/06/making-your-strategy-work-on-t.

18. Zig Ziglar. "101 Inspiring Quotes by Zig Ziglar." *Entrepreneurs Way.* https://medium.com/@entrepreneursway0007/101-inspiring-quotes-by-zig-ziglar-448b8ab66865/

19. Benjamin Franklin. *Goodreads.* 2023 .https://www.goodreads.com/quotes/460142-if-you-fail-to-plan-you-are-planning-to-fail.

20. Justin Donald, "How I Went From 'Golden Handcuffs' Guy To Helping Hundreds of Thousands Ditch the Hamster Wheel for More Wealth and Lifestyle Freedom Today." https://www.lifestyleinvestor.com/about/.

21. Dan Sullivan and Dr. Benjamin Hardy. *The Gap and the Gain: The High Achiever's Guide to Happiness, Confidence, and Success.* (Carlsbad, CA: Hay House, 2021).

22. Prudy Gourguechon. "Entrepreneurs And Suicide Risk: A New Perspective On Entrapment Provides Hope." August 23, 2018. https://www.forbes.com/sites/prudygourguechon/2018/08/23/entrepreneurs-and-suicide-a-new-perspective-on-entrapment-gives-hope/?sh=3e45b7565385.

About the Author

Jeff is a best-selling author, speaker, and business owner. He is the founder of the Oakridge Financial Group, Oakridge Financial Investments, IAPAM (International Association for Physicians in Aesthetic Medicine), Glenmore Healthcare, and Clean Start Weight Loss®.

As a successful serial entrepreneur, Jeff teaches entrepreneurs how to unchain themselves from the daily grind by creating a business that runs without them. *Fire Yourself First* provides a four-step plan to free up your time and allow you to do what you love next.

Jeff has taken his *secret sauce* on how to *analyze, systemize,* and *scale* businesses, and packaged it for you in *Fire Yourself First,* giving you all his strategies and tips so you can unchain yourself from the daily grind.

Fire Yourself First gives you a blueprint to follow that will give you the ability to live the life you aspired to when you started your business. It allows you to step away from the operations of the business while maintaining ownership, working less, and earning much more. *Fire Yourself First* is a mindset that all successful business owners must utilize to *Live a Life Well Lived*, one where *Health, Wealth, and Wellness* are all in balance.

Over the last 20 years, Jeff has taught thousands of people how to start their own businesses. His book, *Clean Start Weight Loss®*, has sold tens of thousands of copies.

Connect at:
FireYourselfFirst.com

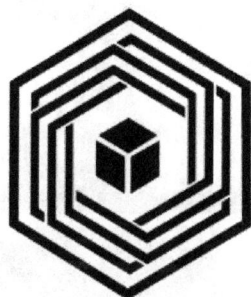

BLOCKCHAIN
VERIFIED IP™

Powered by Easy IP™

CONNECT WITH JEFF

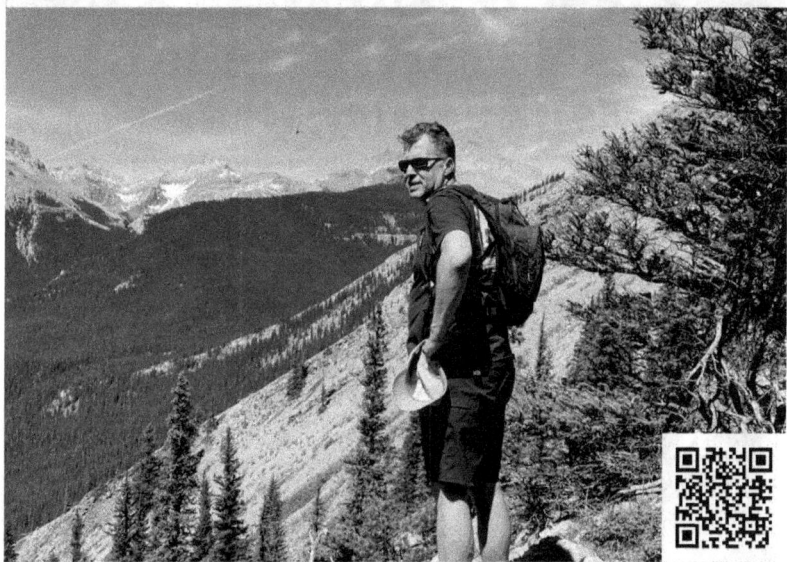

Follow him on your favorite social media platforms today.

FireYourselfFirst.com

Enjoy Jeff's Other Book

SECRETS
—— TO A ——
SUCCESSFUL
PRACTICE

Purpose   Team
SUCCESS
Grow   Track

Strategies for a Successful and
Profitable Cash-Based Medical Practice

JEFF RUSSELL
Executive-Director, IAPAM

AVAILABLE WHEREVER BOOKS ARE SOLD